DEPTH COACHING

DEPTH COACHING

Discovering Archetypes
for Empowerment, Growth, and Balance

PATRICIA R. ADSON, PH.D.

Foreword by Carol S. Pearson, Ph.D.

Gainesville, Florida

Published by the Center for Applications of Psychological Type, Inc.
2815 NW 13th Street, Suite 401
Gainesville FL 32609
352.375.0160
www.capt.org

Center for Applications of Psychological Type, CAPT, and the CAPT logo are trademarks of the Center for Applications of Psychological Type, Inc. in the United States and other countries.

Myers-Briggs Type Indicator, Myers-Briggs, and MBTI are trademarks or registered trademarks of the Myers-Briggs Type Indicator Trust in the United States and other countries.

Organizational and Team Culture Indicator and OTCI are trademarks or registered trademarks of Carol S. Pearson in the United States and other countries.

Pearson-Marr Archetype Indicator and PMAI are trademarks or registered trademarks of Carol S. Pearson and Hugh K. Marr in the United States and other countries.

Printed in the United States of America.

Library of Congress Cataloging-in-Publication Data

Adson, Patricia R.
Depth coaching : discovering archetypes for empowerment, growth, and
balance / Patricia R. Adson.— 1st ed.
        p. cm.
Includes bibliographical references and index.
ISBN 0-935652-76-0
1. Archetype (Psychology) 2. Self-actualization (Psychology) 3. Personal
coaching. I. Title.

BF175.5.A72A37 2004
155.2'64—dc22

2004008725

contents

foreword

LIKE MANY OTHER PEOPLE, I was a coach before coaching was a field. As is apparent from the explanation of my work in *Depth Coaching*, my passion has always been to help people find themselves and in the process discover their gifts and their greatness. I feel so strongly about this because I know that when people contribute their talents in an attitude of service to the greater good—as the Hero does—families, organizations, communities, and whole nations thrive.

The development of coaching as a field provided a name for what I did, but more than that, coaching literature and trainings have expanded my horizons and refined my coaching techniques. I believe that the development of coaching as a profession is critically important. While living one's calling used to be required only for artists, religious leaders, and societal leaders, it is now important for the ordinary person. The problems facing the world are so great that they cannot be addressed solely by a few special people. We *all* need to bring our best and wisest selves to our workplaces, families, and communities.

Not all coaching approaches, however, are equal. Some are, quite frankly, quite shallow. Such approaches merely focus on people's conscious desires and ambitions—which usually comes down to what their egos want or what they have been taught to want—and on supporting them and holding them accountable to implement their goals. As Joseph Campbell warns, many people make the difficult climb up the ladder of success only to find (often later in their lives) that the ladder is leaning against the wrong wall! Depth coaching supports people in going deeper to find what they want at a soul level, not simply what they have been socialized to want.

It is tempting, as coaches, to focus just on what is *in* within the society at the moment and client's sometimes desperate desires to *make it* according to the dictates of the moment. This never really works because by the time the clients have remade themselves to fit the latest fad the world will inevitably have shifted. People will be saying, "been there, done that." In addition, helping people achieve success by pandering to changing societal expectations can never give them what they are genuinely yearning for—the fulfillment that comes from living their purpose.

When people gain enough self-awareness to be guided by their genuine callings and to buttress these commitments with a genuine desire to be of service to the world, the market for what they do generally appears at about the time they have gained mastery in their chosen work. This phenomenon is explained by synchronicity, C. G. Jung's term for "meaningful coincidences." When we are in touch with our deeper selves we simultaneously gain the ability to be in touch with the world.

The individuation process and the archetypes that aid that process are the key to deepening in this way. The book that follows shows coaches how to support this process in their own and in their clients' lives. It is a great honor, therefore, to write this Foreword. I cannot think of a person I would trust more than Dr. Patricia Adson to take theories I developed (in *Awakening the Heroes Within*) about archetypes and the individuation process, integrate them with other theories and models, and apply them to the practice of depth coaching. She has been a valued colleague and friend for many years, and I appreciate the way that her books contribute to helping psychologists, coaches, and others move beyond a focus on health, normality, and shallow definitions of success to bring out the beautiful potential available within each and every human being who comes to them as a client.

Depth Coaching is the second in a series of books by Dr. Adson designed to help professionals use in their work the archetypal theories described in *Awakening the Heroes Within*. The first book, designed for practicing psychotherapists, was *Finding Your Own True North: And Helping Others Find Direction in Life* (Adson, 1999). This incredibly useful book answers the questions, Now that I am a therapist how do I put various theories into practice in a coherent way? and, Now that I am a therapist, what is my role? Adson answered those questions by using the hero's journey model, a combination of Jungian and developmental theory, as a metaphor for the therapeutic process. She then redefined the role of the therapist as that of a journey guide who chooses the therapeutic techniques and interventions appropriate to the tasks the client is attempting to accomplish rather than choosing to work with the particular personality theory or school in which the therapist has been trained.

In *Finding Your Own True North*, Dr. Adson described how she used the archetypes related to the hero's journey in her therapy practice with an extraordinarily beneficial effect on her clients. Now she takes on the field of coaching, answering the analogous questions, Now that I'm a coach, what theory grounds my practice? and Now that I am a coach who must I be? Once again she offers advice to professionals that is wise, seasoned, and proven by the success she has had in her own practice. What I particularly admire about her work is that it combines a theoretically sound approach with real-life examples that give no doubt as to the pragmatism of the approach and its benefit to clients.

Throughout this book, Dr. Adson makes reference to the *Pearson-Marr Archetype Indicator*™ (*PMAI*™) instrument as one means of assessing the archetypes active in clients. Those interested in utilizing the *PMAI* instrument in coaching may want to avail themselves of several supporting publications, including *Introduction to Archetypes* and the *PMAI*™ *Manual*, for more specifics about the use of the instrument. Coaches working with clients who have career or leadership issues may also want to use the *Organizational and Team Culture Indicator*™ (*OTCI*™) instrument to assess the archetypes in the culture of the client's workplace.

These instruments, as well as the material in Dr. Adson's fine book, are equally applicable to *life coaching* (helping people to live the life that suits them), *success coaching* (aiding people in being successful in every area of their lives), and *executive coaching* (assisting leaders and managers to be the best leaders they can be while also finding personal fulfillment). While *Depth Coaching* is written primarily for professionals in the coaching field, the skills and attitudes expressed here can also be helpful to parents, educators, workplace supervisors, and all people charged with helping to develop the full potential of others.

— Carol S. Pearson

Preface

FEW PEOPLE CHOOSE COACHING as their first career; I certainly didn't. In fact I resisted the idea and was rather disdainful and dismissive when articles about personal coaching first began to appear in magazines and newspapers. I knew about executive coaching and sports coaching. I accepted the legitimacy of those endeavors where the sports coach was knowledgeable and experienced in the sport she was coaching and the executive coach was well acquainted with the intricacies of the world of business and management. But *personal life coaching*? As a psychotherapist, I thought personal growth was my territory, and I had worked long and hard to get the qualifications to earn a license.

For some time I remained skeptical. The people who touted coaching often reminded me of motivational speakers, Werner Erhard's est, and other flashy movements—full of style and sometimes getting good results, but lacking substance and not grounded in any particular theory. Although coaching techniques that appeared closely related to sound practices of behavioral theory and other competency-based therapies intrigued me, the promises of health, wealth, and happiness (especially for the coach) sounded slick and superficial.

For several years, however, I had felt increasing pressure to conform my psychotherapy practice to a medical model and system of managed care. This model emphasized mental and emotional distress, ignored soul and spirit, and put me in the role of expert who labeled the client with a diagnosis and applied the approved treatment. I had always been more interested in development than in disease, and for years I had sought ways to work with clients who didn't fit the disease model—ways that emphasized innovation and imagination instead of blame and causation.

In my attempt to treat each client as a unique individual, I found many therapies that appealed to me: brief solution-focused therapy, cognitive behavioral therapy, possibility therapy, and narrative therapy. These *therapeutic approaches* used techniques that addressed competencies and positive qualities. I was also interested in Jungian, existential, and humanistic *theories* that considered meaning and soul and emphasized the uniqueness and complexity of each client. Like most psychotherapists I thought of myself as eclectic and integrative rather than a follower of a particular school. At the same time, I sought a common thread, a basis on which to choose to use these approaches selectively rather than eclectically.

I found that common thread in the developmental framework and conceptual vocabulary of the myth of the *hero's journey* as depicted in the work of Carol S. Pearson. In *Awakening the Heroes Within: Twelve Archetypes to Help Us Find Ourselves and Transform Our World* (1991, 94), Pearson, building on the work of Joseph Campbell and C. G. Jung, identified three phases of the Journey (the Preparation, the Soul Journey, and the Return), explained the relationship of the hero's journey to human development and the therapeutic process, and described twelve archetypes that serve as inner guides on each phase of the journey.

After intensive study with Carol Pearson and years of using this model in my therapeutic practice, I wrote a book called *Finding Your Own True North* (Adson 1999). In this book, I showed therapists how to use the *journey guide/hero's journey* model in the practice of a client-centered therapy using the myth of the hero's journey as a context for the therapy. The therapist could view herself as a journey guide, assume different roles, and integrate various theoretical perspectives depending upon the specific tasks the therapist and client were trying to accomplish rather than the school in which the therapist had been trained.

The hero's journey is a story of development throughout the life span. I saw the therapist/guide as one who helped clients awaken their inherent inner resources to accomplish the developmental tasks of life and find a path of their own. As I continued to work with this concept, however, I realized that as a therapist working within the medical model of psychotherapy and the constraints of managed care, I was primarily restricted to *preparing* people for the journey.

Psychotherapy, with its underpinnings of psychodynamic theory and Freudian thought, is often a reworking of the parental relationship that aids the completion of the developmental tasks of childhood—tasks appropriate to and useful in the basic preparation for the hero's journey. In general, the therapist deals with regression and dysfunction and provides a service often desperately needed. Unquestionably, people who are totally unprepared for the journey and have very little trust or autonomy, or people who have major mental disorders, need a psychotherapist.

For the rest of the journey, however, to become unique individuals and return to share their gifts with the community, clients can use a journey guide. And a journey guide does not have to be a therapist.

As I struggled with my role as a therapist/guide, a therapist friend became interested in the concept of coaching, hired a coach, and began to show me how helpful the process was to her. As she shared her coaching materials and coaching experience with me, I realized that coaches were doing much the same thing I was—working with people to help them find purpose and meaning and discover their own "true north." The process of coaching fit my concept of a journey guide (and the title coach sounded a bit less New Age than journey guide).

When I learned of a program that trained therapists to be coaches (TherapistU, now called The Institute for Life Coach Training), I enrolled to experience coaching first hand. As soon as I read the materials I was impressed. I discovered that coaching is not just about performance but is also about meaning and purpose, vision, plans, taking action, and deepening learning. I realized that as a coach I could move beyond the medical model to become the kind of journey guide I wanted to be.

The TherapistU experience was a new one for me. It was a telephone class where I never met the instructors or the other people in my class. The class was my introduction to distance learning, which I found to be surprisingly effective (as long as the learner is motivated). The course materials and the instructors were excellent, and all of the others in the class were practicing psychologists so the discussions were lively and informative and illuminated the similarities and differences of coaching and psychotherapy.

Eager to learn more about coaching and to meet coaches who came from backgrounds other than therapy, I enrolled in the Hudson Institute of Santa Barbara. The Hudson Institute is a program grounded in theories of adult development and organizational development that emphasize the need to manage change and continually renew oneself in a changing world. Hudson Institute coaches are trained to work with clients not only in the "grand developmental journey through the lifespan" (Hudson and McLean 1996) but also in the life chapters and life transitions of recurring cycles of continuous renewal.

Frederic Hudson, the founder of the Hudson Institute, is an expert on adult development and lifelong learning, and Hudson Institute coaches use a model based on adult developmental theory and a theory of continuous change. I participated in an intense, eight-month-long training experience with forty other people from all over the country. In that group there were only two other mental health professionals, one a psychiatrist and one a clinical social worker. All the others were also highly skilled, mature individuals from law, medicine, the clergy, organizational development, education, hospital administration, management, human resources, and executive positions. We met on common ground in several face-to-face meeting sessions and through phone calls and an Internet bulletin board between sessions.

My work at the Hudson Institute intensified my interest in using the hero's journey model as a basis for a coaching practice: the client as the *hero*, and the coach as a journey guide. In addition, having the opportunity to get to know Pamela McLean, Frederic Hudson, and the staff and trainees of the Hudson Institute reinforced my respect for the caliber of people who are attracted to the field of coaching and coach training.

This book is based on a combination of the work of Carol S. Pearson (in particular *Awakening the Heroes Within* and *The Pearson-Marr Archetype Indicator*® instrument) and the work of the Hudson Institute as presented in Hudson and McLean's *LifeLaunch*. It represents a return from my own professional journey and a continuation (at times a repetition) of the work I began in *Finding Your Own True North*. I have written this book for coaches and other helpers (teachers, parents, supervisors, and counselors) who want to work more intensely with powerful emotions and developmental issues yet retain their professional integrity by not overstepping professional bounds. The book can also serve as a guide for psychotherapists who seek a way to practice a positive psychology based on development rather than disease.

I hope that helpers who want to go "deeper" with clients will find this a useful map of the territory and a source of practical information on which to base a decision to refer a client to a therapist.

I am always interested in hearing from readers regarding their own journeys, about experiences in facilitating the journeys of others, or feedback about using the process outlined in *Depth Coaching*. If you would like to share your experiences, please email me at padson@aol.com.

— PATRICIA R. ADSON

ACKNOWLEDGMENTS

First and foremost this book would not have been possible without the collaboration, the friendship, and the amazing body of work created by Carol S. Pearson. She has enriched my life—professionally and personally—and I am truly grateful.

I am fortunate also to have known and worked with Frederic Hudson, Pamela McLean, the staff of the Hudson Institute of Santa Barbara, and the Hudson Institute coaching community. I am proud to be a Hudson Institute Coach and especially grateful to Minnesota Hudson Institute coaches—Dennis Coyne, Tom Hubler, Bill Lindberg, Elaine Millam, Amy Sayre, Carleton Peterson and Gloria Wallace—great coaches and good friends whose support means more than I can say.

I am indebted to Patrick Williams and Diane Menendez of The Institute for Life Coach Training who first introduced me to the world of responsible professional coaching, and gave me sound advice and wise mentoring as I made the transition from psychologist to coach.

In addition, I want to thank the members of The Edges Learning Community where I continue to learn more about coaching, consciousness, and community and whose founder, Dan Petersen, has been a source of support and encouragement for this book.

I am grateful to editors Susan Mickelberry and Eleanor Sommer for making the book readable, the citations accurate, and for pulling everything together. And a very special thanks to my friend and colleague, Janet Hutton Senjem, for her friendship, her wisdom and her thoughtful comments on this manuscript.

Last, but not least, thanks to my family: my husband, Martin, my children, Judy, Jay, Ted, and especially Jennifer—a fellow Hudson Institute coach and faithful companion on this part of my journey.

INTRODUCTION

THE ROLE OF THE COACH is to enable clients to set their own agendas and help them find the ways or the paths that are right for them. In this book I will introduce a new way to think about the content and the process of coaching—a way that honors each individual while providing an enriching model of adult development that draws upon the work of Jung, Erik Erikson, and Carol S. Pearson. This new way to look at coaching is certainly not the *only* way, but it is one that works well for me as I help clients deal with the deeper issues of emotional, social, and spiritual development without trespassing into the territory of psychotherapy. I call this process *depth coaching*.

THE HERO'S JOURNEY:
THE CONTEXT OF DEPTH COACHING

Coaching as a discipline is a client-centered way of working with individuals to help them achieve their goals, balance their lives, and attain fulfillment. Coaching focuses on clients' lifelong development rather than the remediation of past wounds. Coach and client collaborate as partners or peers in a relationship that is symmetric rather than paternalistic.

The agenda in a coaching relationship is determined by the client, not the coach, and the coaching client is considered "naturally whole and resourceful" rather than dysfunctional or disordered. Coaching differs from psychotherapy, where the focus is on the treatment of personality problems, maladjustments and mental disorders. The territory of the coach is that of adult development, whereas the territory of the psychotherapist is more likely to involve the uncompleted tasks of child development. Coaching is a process of enrichment rather than repair.

I define depth coaching as an approach to coaching that focuses on unconscious mental processes as the source of emotional, physical, mental, and spiritual well-being, in contrast to depth psychology, which views these unconscious mental processes as the source of emotional disturbance and distress.[1] The depth coach helps people retrieve innate inner resources from the depths of the unconscious to help them deal with the challenges and transitions of adult life and find their places in the world.

To understand these complex issues of adult development, growth, and change, I use the myth of the hero's journey as a theoretical foundation and to provide a simple map of the territory of human development. Using this model we can also consider Erik Erikson's psychosocial developmental tasks, adult developmental theory, and Jungian thought within the same framework.

The Stages of the Journey

The myth of the hero's journey provides a map that shows the integration of various developmental theories and enables us to consider all of these elements as a coherent whole. The myth applies to every adult and tells the universal story of human development—the natural history of our species. Each person recapitulates the journey many times—longitudinally (across the life span) and cyclically (within phases of our lives). Every time we leave the familiar behind, we begin a new journey. Every life transition is a potential journey.

In the myth, the hero prepares for the journey by learning to care for himself or herself, takes the journey by fighting *dragons* and discovering unique *treasures*, and then returns to share these treasures with the *kingdom*. It is the story of preparation, separation, and return, of dependence, independence, and interdependence—the natural cycles of life.

Now the myth of the hero's journey is not a myth in the sense that it is untrue but in the sense that myths originated as a "shared cultural context for communication . . . ways of teaching unobservable realities by way of observable symbols" (Hampden-Turner 1982, 198). The task of the hero is to claim one's own life and place in the world instead of having one's life and place in the world determined by others.[2] In his classic *The Hero With a Thousand Faces*, Joseph Campbell brought this timeless myth to public awareness and made people realize that each of us can be a hero as long as we are free to choose and capable of change.

In *Awakening the Heroes Within*, Pearson described the relationship of the hero's journey and archetypal inner resources to the development of Ego, Soul, and Self—the three stages of the hero's journey (figure 1.1). She described the first stage, Preparation (Ego), as the time when the hero prepares to leave a state of dependence and develop the inner resources necessary to go forth into the world on his or her own. Pearson identified the second stage, the Soul Journey (Soul), as the period when the hero discovers the *gifts* that constitute the true and independent self. The third stage, the Return (Self), refers to a time when the hero returns to the community to share these gifts and live with others in a state of interdependence.

Erikson's Psychosocial Stages

Pearson noted the correlation of the stages of the journey to the developmental stages Erik Erikson identified when he related Freud's psycho*sexual* stages to the psycho*social* stages of life and named the developmental tasks presented by each stage of life (Erikson 1963). Erikson's psychosocial stages are indicated in figure 1.2.

Figure 1.3 shows the relationship of Erikson's developmental tasks to the stages of the journey as described by Pearson. We can use this as a coherent mental map of the breadth and the depth of the human adventure.

Figure 1.1 The stages of the hero's journey

Stage one
Preparation for separation—dependence
Ego-building
ELEMENTS: the Call, the Fall, wounds, facing the Dragons

Stage two
The Journey to find the individual—independence—Soul-finding
ELEMENTS: fighting the Dragons and finding the treasure

Stage three
The Return to community—interdependence—Self-responsibility
ELEMENTS: sharing the treasure with others

Figure 1.2 Erik Erikson's psychosocial stages

Infancy
Trust vs. mistrust

Early childhood
Autonomy vs. doubt and shame

Preschool
Initiative vs. guilt

School age
Industry vs. inferiority

Adolescence
Identity vs. role confusion

Young adulthood
Intimacy vs. isolation

Middle age
Generativity vs. stagnation

Later life
Integrity vs. despair

(Erikson 1963)

About Archetypes

"The idea of archetypes is an ancient one. It is related to Plato's concept of ideal forms: patterns already existing in the divine mind that determine in what form the material world will come into being. But we owe to Jung the concept of the psychological archetypes: the characteristic patterns that pre-exist in the collective psyche of the human race, that repeat themselves eternally in the psyches of individual human beings and determine the basic ways that we perceive and function as psychological beings."

— Robert Johnson
Inner Work

Jung's idea of psychological archetypes was a departure from the theories of Sigmund Freud. Freud believed that children came into the world as blank slates whose personalities were developed by interactions with their parents. He used the myth of Oedipus to demonstrate the way a child's personality evolved and to explain how the child could be scarred by sexually charged events in the parent-child relationship.

Jung, on the other hand, believed that the Oedipus myth represented only one aspect or element of human development. While Jung agreed that personal experience played a part in individual development, he also believed that we came into the world with a common psychic substrate—patterns of instinctual behavior available to all. For Jung, the role of personal experience was to develop and awaken innate inner abilities that already existed—the archetypes of the collective unconscious and the personal unconscious. Unlike Freud, who viewed the personal unconscious as a mass of instinctual and repressed desires (usually sexual), Jung saw the unconscious as hidden treasures waiting to be explored.

Pearson's Archetypes

"We are aided on our journey by inner guides, or archetypes, each of which exemplifies a way of being on the journey . . . Each has a lesson to teach us, and presides over a stage of the journey."

— Carol Pearson
Awakening the Heroes Within

In *Awakening the Heroes Within*, Pearson helped us work more easily with the nebulous, abstract concept of archetypes by personifying the archetypes inherent in the human developmental process. She identified these archetypes as inner guides that are available to guide each hero (person) through the three stages of the journey. Rather than use unfamiliar Latin, Greek, or psychological terms for these aspects of our personalities, Pearson called them by recognizable names—the Innocent, the Orphan, the Warrior, the Caregiver, the Lover, the Seeker,

Figure 1.3 Pearson's stages of the journey and Erikson's psychosocial stages and tasks

---

Preparation
Ego development—dependence

TRUST
task = developing trust in self and others

AUTONOMY
task = standing up for, protecting, and defending the self

INITIATIVE
task = learning to take responsibility for self

INDUSTRY
task = learning basic social skills and work habits

Journey
Soul—identity—independence

IDENTITY
task = finding what you love, creating, and letting go

INTIMACY
task = finding whom you love, willingness to commit and let go

---

Return
Self—wholeness—interdependence

GENERATIVITY
task = actively sharing your gifts with others

INTIMACY
task = being true to yourself and claiming your own wisdom

Figure 1.4 Brief descriptions of Pearson's twelve archetypes

Archetypes of the Preparation Stage of the Journey

The INNOCENT—the pure and trusting part of us that retains faith regardless of personal experience

The ORPHAN—the part that has been betrayed, abused, or abandoned

The CAREGIVER—the ability to nurture and care for others and ourselves

The WARRIOR—the ability to protect and defend ourselves and set limits and goals

Archetypes of the Soul Journey

The SEEKER—the need to search for something different, seek meaning, explore, and wander

The LOVER—the ability to care, to bond, to make commitments, and to have passion

The CREATOR—the ability to open the imagination and bring forth something that never existed before

The DESTROYER—the ability to choose to let go and rid yourself of things that no longer support your values; also, the acceptance of mortality

Archetypes of the Return

The RULER—the ability to use all of our resources and to take responsibility for ourselves and for others

The SAGE—the ability to attain wisdom, seek truth, and tolerate ambiguity

The MAGICIAN—the ability to change what needs to be changed by acting on our own visions

The JESTER—the ability to experience life fully and to tell the truth with impunity

the Creator, the Destroyer, the Ruler, the Sage, the Magician, and the Jester/Fool.[3] (In later work, Pearson modified the name Fool, changing it to Jester.) Figure 1.4 gives brief descriptions of each of these aspects.

These archetypes are names given to basic human resources, traits, and capabilities that are built into the biological substrate of human beings. They are ways to categorize and talk about our capacity to care for others, to stand up for and defend ourselves, to feel wonder and trust, and to experience a sense of loss (among many other things). We call on the archetypes to accomplish the fundamental tasks of human development, such as learning to trust, to be autonomous, to find our identity and our work, and to live in integrity and pass on what we have learned to others. In doing this, we take the hero's journey (metaphorically), fight our dragons (other people's expectations for us), find our treasures and our identity, and return to share these with the community.

The archetypal resources live in each one of us and can be activated, developed, awakened, or called forth at various stages and ages of our lives. However, although archetypes are universal, innate predispositions, they will appear a little differently to each person because they are filtered through our culture and life experiences.[4]

We can learn to evoke and to balance these forces only after we have acknowledged their presence. Becoming aware of archetypal forces allows us to activate these inner resources and to live intentional lives, lives that we compose and manage ourselves. When we are unaware of the archetypes, they "live us" instead of our living them. By this I mean that when we are unaware our behavior is driven by forces that we don't know we can control. As a result, our reactions to stimuli are unconscious and immature. Adding the archetypes to the stages of the journey and developmental tasks, as represented in figure 1.5, completes the map of the territory of development and change.

The archetypes are inner resources we can call on to make our ways through the terrain—to guide us on our journeys. Therapists and coaches can help clients find their ways when they are lost or uncertain and also guide them to an awareness of meaning and purpose that enables them to make contributions to the world.

HOW TO READ THIS BOOK

A guide doesn't guide by telling you *about* the journey. She helps you to explore your life and get the most out of it in your own way. Because coaches can't help others experience something that has only been described in a book, I'll invite you, the reader, to take a journey of your own. Read this book as if you were taking your own journey. Ask yourself the questions and do the exercises as you read through the body of the book.

I will take you on the journey of the coach and tell you a little bit about my own journey as we go. As you read the sections on the Ego and the Soul, you will experience what it is like to prepare for and take your personal journey and become familiar with the hero's journey vocabulary as a context for depth coaching. In the section on the Return, you will integrate what you have learned about yourself into your professional journey and see how the *journey guide five-step process* can help organize your interactions with your clients in the coaching process.

As you take your journey, you may find it helpful to refer to the Comprehensive Map in figure 1.6 (page 6). The map integrates the archetypes with the developmental theories I have touched upon in this introduction. If you choose to take a more intensive journey, I have included a workbook for each section of the journey at the end of each chapter. Please read the workbook even if you don't plan to take an extensive journey right now. The exercises in the workbook can also be used in your work with your clients.

As you read this material and work with the process of the hero's journey, you may notice some words that are unfamiliar to you or that are used in unfamiliar ways. A brief glossary is provided on page 115 to assist you in incorporating these new meanings into your study of depth coaching.

Now, listen for the *call*, take the journey, awaken the archetypes, slay the dragons, find

Figure 1.5 Stages of the journey, Erikson's psychosocial stages and Pearson's archetypes

Preparation *Ego development—dependence*	Archetypes
TRUST	Innocent
AUTONOMY	Orphan
INITIATIVE	Caregiver
INDUSTRY	Warrior

Journey *Soul—identity—independence*	Archetypes
IDENTITY	Seeker
INTIMACY	Lover
	Creator
	Destroyer

Return *Self—wholeness—interdependence*	Archetypes
GENERATIVITY	Ruler
INTIMACY	Sage
	Magician
	Jester

the treasures, and return to your particular kingdom. Bon voyage, and remember the immortal words of Yogi Berra: "It *ain't over* 'til it's over." The journey isn't over until the hero returns and shares her treasures with the kingdom.

Notes

1. *Longman Dictionary of Psychology and Psychiatry* defines depth psychology as "a general approach to psychology and psychotherapy that focuses on *unconscious mental processes as a source of emotional disturbance and symptoms* (my italics), as well as personality, attitudes, creativity, and style of life. A classic example is Freudian psychoanalysis, but others, notably Jung, Adler, Horney, and Sullivan, employed a depth approach" (Goldenson 1984, 214).

2. "Hannah Arendt in *The Human Condition* cites the distinction that the ancient Greek philosophers made between 'animal' work—the work of a slave or a woman (an *animal laborans*, or laboring animal), necessary to

Figure 1.6 Comprehensive Map

Stage of the Journey	Preparation	Soul Journey	Return
	EGO	SOUL	SELF
Archetypes	Innocent Orphan Caregiver Warrior	Seeker Lover Destroyer Creator	Ruler Sage Magician Jester
Outcome	Caring for the self Getting along with others	Finding your gifts, values, purpose, and identity	Sharing your gifts with others Living in integrity
Developmental Tasks	Trust Autonomy	Identity Intimacy	Generativity Integrity
Elements of the Journey	Wounds Ego and Skill development	The call and the fall Dragons Gifts, values and purpose	Integration of the Ego and Soul Sharing treasures with the world

stay alive but leaving no mark behind, sweeping the floor that gets dirty again, cooking the meal that gets eaten—and 'human' work. Human work, to those Greeks, the work of free men, involved courage: the risk of casting one's own being into the arena, in art, political contest, or any game of human skill in which you make your individual mark on your time. The concept of 'hero' comes from that definition of 'human work.' Originally, it did not necessarily connote great physical bravery but simply the risk of freely chosen tasks or adventure in a community of equals, in which you dared to expose your true self" (Freidan 1993).

3. To learn more about each of the archetypes, see *Awakening the Heroes Within* (249).

4. Pearson (1991, 6) explains: "Because the guides are truly archetypal, and hence reside as energy within the unconscious psychological life of all people everywhere, they exist both inside and outside the individual human soul. They live in us, but even more importantly, we live in them. We can, therefore, find them by going inward (to our own dreams, fantasies, and often actions as well) or by going outward (to myth, legend, art, literature, and religion, and, as pagan cultures often did, to the constellations of the sky and the birds and animals of the earth). Thus, they provide images of the hero within and beyond ourselves."

Chapter One

TAKING THE COACH'S JOURNEY

BUILDING THE BLOCKS OF THE EGO			
The Innocent	The Orphan	The Caregiver	The Warrior

"The Ego is the seat of consciousness, the recognition that there is an 'I' separate from the mother and the rest of the world, an 'I' that can affect that world. The mature adult Ego develops its capabilities in order to fulfill all our needs, not just the need for safety. . . . It also balances our individual needs with the needs of others, and in that way contributes to the survival and development of the individual, the family, the community, the nation, and the species."

— CAROL PEARSON
Awakening the Heroes Within

WE CAN HELP OURSELVES and others prepare for the journey by revisiting the developmental tasks of childhood and balancing the archetypes of the ego. The ego archetypes are the basic building blocks of the human experience; they are our internal representation of the mother-father-child triad that appear as recurring themes in art, myth, poetry, and literature. To prepare for the journey is to develop the ego strength that ultimately allows us to move from a state of dependency to a state of independence and to maintain that state as we travel on.

In psychological terms the ego is described as "the component of the personality that deals with the external world and its practical demands . . . [and] enables us to perceive, reason, solve problems, test reality, and adjust instinctual impulses . . . at the behest of the conscious . . ." (Goldenson 1984, 247). The ego plays the important role of "maintaining balance between inner impulses and outer reality" (249). Before we set off on the journey, our first task is to review the Ego archetypes and make sure that all the necessary resources are available.

In terms of human development, it is easy to understand that before we can become independent we have to establish trust, autonomy, industry, and initiative (Erik Erikson's developmental tasks of childhood). If we don't develop these we might be forced to rely on other people and institutions for our care—or at least for a sense of who we are. People who have not developed a *basic* level of trust or autonomy, and therefore have what might be called exceptionally low ego strength, are more likely to be candidates for psychotherapy than for coaching. However, most people, and certainly most clients who choose a coach instead of a therapist, have developed enough trust and independence to survive and do quite well in the adult world. Even so, it is good to review the Ego archetypes and become aware of the more subtle ways in which we remain dependent on the approval or the direction of others and the damaging effects this can have on our living life to the fullest.

THE MAJOR DEVELOPMENTAL TASKS FOR THE PREPARATION

The first major developmental task for the preparation of the journey is the development of basic trust in yourself that you will be able to survive and care for yourself. The second is development of autonomy—the ability to care for yourself. Erikson's tasks of industry and initiative are also important but will not be considered separately here.

Readiness for the Journey

You recognize that you aren't fully prepared for the journey when you find yourself continually doing things so others will like you or think that you're okay. Other signs that you are unprepared for the journey may include being unable to delegate and feeling you must run your whole office by yourself, being afraid to say what you think because someone might get angry, or being afraid to leave a relationship or a job for fear that you can't make it on your own. Or you may realize that you are taking care of everyone in your family or office except yourself. None of these issues indicate character flaws or insurmountable obstacles; they merely indicate that you haven't

fully completed the developmental tasks of learning to trust in yourself and to stand up for yourself (autonomy). That is why the preparation work almost always starts with the Ego. Most of us have work to do to prepare for the deeper and more demanding elements of the journey.

As you do this ego work, it is good to let go of the negative ideas you may have heard about the ego. Don't worry—having a well-balanced ego is not being egotistical or selfish. On the journey and beyond you will continue to care about other people's opinions and reactions and want approval. At the same time you will know that you can (and must) trust yourself to take care of yourself and handle authority in yourself and in others.

THE INNOCENT ARCHETYPE

The part that trusts life, ourselves, and other people.

GIFTS
Trust, optimism, loyalty.

ASK YOURSELF . . .
Do I know when to trust others and when not to? How can I learn to trust myself?

"The Innocent is the part of us that trusts life, ourselves, and other people. It is the part that has faith and hope, even when on the surface things look impossible."

— CAROL S. PEARSON
Awakening the Heroes Within

Think of Winnie the Pooh. Pooh Bear is certain that every pot is full of honey and that every pot of honey is waiting, just for him. Pooh knows the world loves him and that things will always work out for the best. Did a smile come to your face as your mind wandered back to the gentle world of Pooh? That smile, or the automatic smile evoked by the sight of a happy child or a puppy, is a natural response to the Innocent archetype

The Innocent has trust and faith and optimism. Some of us begin our training in a helping profession as Innocents with exceptionally high ideals and aspirations. We believe that if we work hard enough and do things right we will be able to help others and make a contribution to the world. The idea of becoming a coach, guide, or therapist is especially attractive to the innocent part of us that believes that others share our high ideals and good motives.

Complete innocence isn't enough. The unbalanced Innocent places her trust in *others* instead of *herself* and ignores and denies the facts. Recall the ultimate innocence of the comic strip character Charlie Brown who year after year trusted Lucy to hold the football and year after year was betrayed. Do you find yourself returning again and again to the same situation, believing that this time it will be different? Do you believe people even when their actions don't match their sincere sounding words? When that happens, stop and acknowledge the Innocent and then begin to work with facts, not faith alone.

Sandra's journey. Let's follow Sandra as she prepares for her journey as a coach. Sandra, a highly skilled sales manager, considered herself a people person. Co-workers came to her for advice and counsel about their personal lives. She was well liked and fun to be around but her heart wasn't in her job. She was an eager follower of new age theories, had complete trust that the "universe will provide," and had unlimited optimism. At an inspirational workshop she met a charismatic coach and realized she didn't belong in the world of commerce. Impulsively, she quit her office job and enrolled in a coach-training program.

The Innocent is quite wonderful but cannot take the journey alone or she will end up like Little Red Riding Hood. Innocence and trust are lovely qualities that all of us would do well to cultivate. However, when innocence is not balanced by some of the Orphan's skepticism, the Warrior's realism, and the Caregiver's concern, we are apt to be overly trusting of authority figures and vulnerable to believing everything we are told. Every new scheme will look like the

answer to all of life's problems. Total Innocents tend to worship at the foot of the guru and follow the guru's path instead of their own. The innocence of a child is a beautiful thing to behold, and we should do everything we can to protect it, but an adult who remains in complete innocence (the *shadow* Innocent) denies her own experience, lives in a state of dependency, and drinks the poison Kool-Aid.

THE ORPHAN ARCHETYPE

The part that has faced the fall, betrayal, abuse, or abandonment.

GIFTS
Interdependence, empathy, and realism.

ASK YOURSELF . . .
Do I feel abandoned or rejected by others when they don't agree with me? Do I orphan myself by ignoring my own feelings?

"When the Orphan is dominant in our lives, the world seems a pretty hopeless place. We have been abandoned by whatever parental figure might rescue us and are left with a landscape inhabited by two kinds of people: the weak who are victims, and the strong, who either ignore or victimize the weak."
— CAROL PEARSON
Awakening the Heroes Within

At the extreme levels of the archetypes, the opposite of the Innocent is the Orphan. Return again for a minute to Pooh's land of the Hundred Acre Wood and recall the character of Eeyore, the Old Grey Donkey. Eeyore groans that "nobody minds and nobody cares." On the map of the "hundred acker wood," Eeyore's home is called "Eeyore's gloomy place" and described as "rather boggy and sad" (Milne 1926). If you hang your head, allow your shoulders to droop, and repeat Eeyore's lament, "nobody minds and nobody cares," you will experience the archetype of the total Orphan who is seriously out of balance with the other archetypal energies.

The unbalanced Orphan always feels like a victim and frequently blames others when things go wrong. Often we will see him as the person who decided to become a coach or a therapist hoping that the training would heal a wound or take the place of psychotherapy. Certainly victims of abuse may need therapy and support, but ultimately we all need to learn to take care of ourselves (particularly if we want to help others), and the unbalanced Orphan hasn't learned this yet.

We all experience orphaning at some points in our lives. Orphaning comes with the loss of innocence and is a bewildering experience. A betrayed wife says, "I've done everything right in this marriage. I've been faithful, a good mother, a companion, and a homemaker, and now he is leaving." The cancer patient says, "I have taken care of myself all my life, exercised, and eaten properly. I don't smoke or drink. What is going on? I can't cope with this." These people have indeed been orphaned, and being orphaned is seldom the orphan's fault.

Sandra's journey continued. Well before Sandra completed her training program she began to feel discouraged. She didn't complete the assignments and complained bitterly to anyone who would listen when the course director refused to make exceptions and asked her to repeat some of the classes. In a few months, Sandra had moved from a position of the total Innocent to a low-level Orphan. She felt orphaned by the coach-training program that had promised her so much, and she orphaned herself by lashing out at others and not examining her own feelings and responsibilities. Sandra decided to quit.

Our Orphan self is our most vulnerable part. The Innocent and the Orphan are child-like and defenseless, and as we struggle to meet all of the demands of adult life and responsibility we often ignore our own Orphans (our vulnerable parts) and pretend to be invulnerable. When we forget our Orphan we essentially abandon—orphan—ourselves.

Coaches can lose the ability to connect with scared and sensitive clients when they don't know how to connect with those parts of themselves.

Such coaches are likely to view displays of emotion in themselves and in others as weakness or illness and to become authoritarian rather than compassionate. Evidence is growing that empathic relationships are more conducive to health than any other form of social support and that to support the feeling states of others we must have experienced those states ourselves (Bakal 1999). The gift of the Orphan is the ability to fully experience emotional states that, in turn, enable us to empathize with others. The Orphan shows us how to join together with others, to recognize that we are all wounded, flawed, and vulnerable in some ways. The Orphan enables us to give and also to *receive* support.

The Metaphor of the Inner Child

The Innocent child believes that the world revolves around her: the Orphan child feels alienated and abandoned by the world. Together, the Innocent and the Orphan represent the *inner child*, the most primitive of our archetypes, or the youngest part of our being, which experiences emotions, needs care and approval, and is unable to care for itself. These two archetypes (or this metaphoric inner child) need *inner parents* or inner adults to care for and protect them and help them make choices about their behaviors. For those tasks, we call on the Caregiver and the Warrior.

THE CAREGIVER ARCHETYPE

The part that nurtures and cares for ourselves and others.

GIFTS
Compassion and generosity.

ASK YOURSELF . . .
What does it mean to care for myself emotionally and physically? What is my life like when I am taking good care of myself?

"The ideal of the Caregiver is the perfect, caring parent—generative, loving, attentive to noticing and developing the child's talents and interest,

so devoted to this new life that he or she would die, if necessary, that it might thrive."

— CAROL PEARSON
Awakening the Heroes Within

———————

"The myth of the Caregiver is the story of the transformative quality of giving and even, at times, of sacrifice."

— CAROL PEARSON
Awakening the Heroes Within

———————

You can evoke the level of the Caregiver who cares for others by recalling positive images, experiences, or memories of parents and children. For instance, recall a Renaissance painting of the Madonna and Child, bring back a memory of sitting by the bedside of a child who is afraid or ill, or recall a time when you rocked a child to sleep, read *Goodnight Moon*, or made a peanut butter and jelly sandwich for a hungry three-year-old.

Although it is easy to evoke the felt sense of the archetype with images or experiences of one person caring for another, the image or experience of caring for the self is harder to call forth. For many, it is easier to give than to receive, and much easier to give to others than to the self.

To experience the Caregiver, fold your arms gently across your chest and for a moment embrace yourself. Allow yourself to experience being held and cared for. This calls forth the part of the Caregiver archetype that cares for the self. We become aware of our obligation for self-care when we learn to take good care of our physical bodies and fully realize that no one else can do this for us. Usually, we can activate the part of an internal parent who sees that we get enough sleep and exercise, eat properly, and keep ourselves clean. Emotional care of the self, however, is far more difficult to picture and put into action.

We need our Caregiver archetype for emotional self-care whenever we are signaled or alerted by emotions of fear, sadness, guilt, or shame. Without access to the internal Caregiver we look outside (to someone else) for comfort or reassurance. We seek some parental figure to

make it all right. Other times we tell ourselves that there is something wrong with feeling the way we do. In the example above, Sandra was trying to get the training program to take care of her and change their requirements so that she would feel better. She argued her case to everyone who would listen, hoping to enlist sympathy and allies. She believed she was being victimized and betrayed.

Think of a time when your feelings were hurt or you felt insulted or "put down." How did you handle the situation? If you told yourself you shouldn't feel that way, or if you lashed out at someone, or spiraled down into a black mood, that was a time you needed to call on the Caregiver.

The person with easy access to the Caregiver archetype will continue to want allies and support but at the same time will also be capable of looking inside herself for help. We care for ourselves by acknowledging and experiencing our emotions, not judging them, denying them, or trying to make them go away. We understand that our emotions are telling us something about ourselves, not about someone else. We care for ourselves by soothing ourselves, the way a mother soothes a child. When a child is afraid of thunder and lightning, the parent who says, "Don't be afraid," isn't soothing the child. She is denying the child's emotions. The parent who says, "I can see that you are scared, and I'll stay with you," is soothing the child. When a child has an angry outburst the parent who says, "Don't be angry," is not soothing or care-giving the child. The parent who says, "I can see that you are angry, and I'll help you decide what you need to do about it," provides the child with an experience of the Caregiver. Remember that emotions are perfectly natural, not symptoms of illness, and don't need to be ignored, avoided, made to "go away," or even (at times) expressed to other people. Emotions need to be acknowledged—and not with mindless platitudes from ourselves or others.

The Caregiver archetype helps us to attend to the physical and emotional signals we experience. And learning self-soothing and bodily awareness enables us to do our part in maintaining the physical balance essential to our well-being. Self-soothing is one of the most important of life skills and is not to be confused with pampering the self. Once we learn to soothe the self with empathic self-support, we can reap the physical and emotional benefits of social support so essential to good health and recovery from illness.

The Caregiver represents our capacity to love and care for each other and ourselves. Without this most "sublime of all the archetypes," the species could not survive. People in helping professions call on this archetype frequently. They must learn to honor and respect the Caregiver. At the same time, professionals must always be aware that on the Caregiver's shadow side (the unbalanced Caregiver out of touch with other archetypes) lurks the martyr who sacrifices herself for others. In so doing, she helps neither and may even prevent others from learning how to care for themselves.

Professionals who coach or counsel others can take care of their own emotions by acknowledging their emotions, being aware of what moves them, and being conscious of situations that make them uncomfortable. Coaching others at a deeper level requires the capacity to differentiate the personal, internal emotional states of the coach from those of the clients. Professionals must remain aware that their role is not to express or care for their own emotional states, but to help clients learn to care for themselves.

Do you find yourself wanting to take care of your clients' feelings by withholding feedback that might upset them, or by not holding them accountable to their stated goals? Observe yourself and ask if you are *caretaking* instead of *caregiving*. Remember that taking care of others' feelings is just as bad as asking them to take care of yours. Remember that coaches, guides, or helpers deal with functioning adults who are capable of disagreeing with us and expressing and acting on their own feelings. Unlike therapists, coaches do not deal with the vulnerable, the ill, or the immature. Again, coaches are not substitutes for parents.

_____

Sandra's journey continued. Fortunately Sandra's coach, Joe, is a high-level Caregiver coach who trusts his clients' ability to learn to take care of themselves. Joe doesn't try to be a lecturing or a comforting parent. He helps clients integrate the mind that thinks and the mind that feels (the heart and the head) and shows them how to use emotional intelligence "to motivate oneself, and persist in the face of frustration; to control impulse and delay gratification; to regulate one's moods and keep distress from swamping the ability to think; to empathize and to hope" (Goleman 1995, 34). That is, he helps his clients to evoke the Ego archetypes to prepare themselves for the journey.

_____

Although some thought Sandra might need psychotherapy, Joe, recalling her original enthusiasm, wondered if he might first try to help her prepare for her journey by inviting her to experience and learn some emotional self-care. He asked her if she would be willing to try some work on self-care and decided that if they made no progress he would refer her to a therapist. Sandra agreed. When Sandra told Joe of her disappointment and her decision to quit, he began by empathizing with her. Then he directed her attention back to a deeper, more intense, experience of the feeling. He didn't allow her to orphan herself by abandoning her own feelings and focusing all of her attention on what others were doing. Through a series of powerful questions and experiential exercises, Joe helped Sandra identify her feelings and discover what these feelings might be telling her about herself rather than about the training program and the instructors. Sandra began to turn inward and listen to herself like a caring parent, not fleeing from her own fears, anger, and disappointment, but simply acknowledging their presence.

Notice that the coach did not take over the role of Caregiver (as we are sometimes tempted to do) but instead enabled Sandra to evoke a Caregiver of her own.

That was a good first step, but no matter how skilled the Caregiver, she can't go it alone or we would treat ourselves as we would a small defenseless child who needs to be sheltered from the world. We need to be able to act on our feelings, stand firm, express ourselves, and defend our autonomy in the world, and for that we call on the Warrior.

THE WARRIOR ARCHETYPE

The part that has courage, strength, and the ability to make goals, set limits, and fight for the self.

GIFTS
Courage, discipline, and skill.

ASK YOURSELF . . .
How do I go about determining my goals and my limits? How do I stand up for myself? In what ways do I protect and defend myself?

"The Warrior within each of us calls us to have courage, strength, and integrity; the capacity to make goals and stick to them; and the ability to fight, when necessary, for ourselves or others. . . . Warrioring is about claiming our power in the world. . . ."

— CAROL PEARSON
Awakening the Heroes Within

We claim the Warrior to accomplish the developmental tasks of developing autonomy and industry. Remember how wonderful it felt as a small child to be tucked into bed and read a story by loving parents, and how much fun you had on family picnics or trips to the beach? But recall also that when you were a teenager you didn't want these very same parents to cross the threshold of your bedroom, and the thought of going on a family outing felt more like a punishment than a reward. Pearson says, "As long as we are in a child ego state, having boundaries set by others for our benefit and with our interests in mind makes us feel safe and secure (as long as they are not really too oppressive). However, when we are ready to become more autonomous, suddenly those rules and restrictions seem much less benign" (Pearson 1991, 100).

The Warrior is our internal sense of authority that enables us to deal realistically with other authority figures in the world instead of viewing every supervisor, manager, teacher, minister, counselor, or mate as a representative of a stern parent.

You know you lack the Warrior when you are afraid to stand up for yourself, when you see every boss as a tyrant who doesn't know how to run an office, when you can't set goals or limits and stick to them. You know you have an unbalanced Warrior when you are aggressive rather than assertive, and especially when you have a strong need to be right in all things. You claim the Warrior and become autonomous by taking responsibility for your own actions—by speaking up for yourself, setting your own limits and holding to them, and protecting yourself from intrusions from others. The Warrior knows when and how to compete and when and how to call on the Caregiver to cooperate with others.

To experience the Warrior archetype, place your arms outstretched directly in front of you with your palms facing forward. Stand tall, look straight ahead, and say firmly, "No!" Feel the strength of your position and the certainty with which you claim authority. Allow yourself to feel the Warrior when you have to set limits with an employee, or a spouse, or a child having a temper tantrum (and must do this even though the child may say, "I hate you," and the employee will disagree strongly with your decision).

Recognize that the setting of limits is setting limits on yourself. When working with the parents of troubled children, counselors and therapists help these parents determine their own limits before they attempt to set limits on the child. They ask the parents, "What are you willing to do? How often do you need to take a break? What behaviors will you tolerate? Where will you draw the line?" Each of us is ultimately in control of our own limits, not those of others. Know what you are going to do if someone crosses your line in the sand—and then, do it!

The depth coach has a well-balanced Warrior who knows her or his own limits and personal boundaries and respects the boundaries of others. She doesn't force clients to talk about things they don't want to talk about. She runs her business in a professional way and holds her clients accountable to their own goals.

Many people burn out or get physically ill before they realize that they have the authority and the ability to set limits. I once had a coaching relationship with a marvelous coach who was outstanding in every way but one: she hadn't balanced her Warrior and Caregiver. She had a difficult time managing her very busy schedule, didn't know how to say "no," frequently missed coaching calls, and kept poor records. Her Caregiver archetype was in martyr mode caring for all the others in her life and neglecting herself. Her outside life reflected the lack of inner balance and harmony. A realignment of the Caregiver and the Warrior helped this coach to regain equilibrium. Her own personal coach made her aware of her need for inner balance by suggesting that she create several scenarios for her future including the most desired outcome and one that involved the consequences of not making any changes in her practice. She pictured herself becoming ill and not being able to take care of others and saw that she would need to set her personal limits and assert herself by saying "yes" to the self. When she pictured the consequences (and especially the benefits) of saying "yes" to the self, she was able to do this.

Pearson explains that saying "yes" to the self is taking the hero's journey. When we say "yes" to the self, we call on the Warrior archetype. Many of us find it difficult to say "no," and coaches and therapists will often assign their clients the task of saying "no" several times in the next week. For some clients, that exercise may not be enough; for once we have said "no" we have to go deeper and call on the Warrior archetype to help us stand fast and endure the discomfort of not pleasing others. When clients are hesitant to say "no" to someone, I often ask them if there is any part of the request or anything else they *are* willing to do for that person.

Raymond's journey. As Raymond thought about an upcoming visit from a grown son he shook his head and said, "You know, I'm not really looking forward to this, because I know he is going to ask me for money, and I don't know what to say. I have the money but I want to use it to take some trips, and I know that will sound selfish to him." (This is living from the outside in. Recognize this?)

I asked him if there was any amount of money he was willing to give or lend, or if there was another way he was truly willing to help. He examined his finances and came up with a plan he felt good about (it wasn't necessary for me to know how much or what he was going to give). He then rehearsed his statement to his son aloud and in writing. By making a statement of what he was willing to do, he claimed his authority (his Warrior) and didn't react defensively, explain, or try to stave off a request that he wasn't willing to fulfill.

Other people don't always like it when we claim our authority, but the Warrior reminds us that we are responsible for our actions, not other people's reactions. We might do well to keep this as a mantra and repeat it again and again.

Sandra's journey continued. When Sandra lashed out and openly criticized her training program, she thought she was being assertive. In reality she was neither protecting, nor defending, nor taking responsibility for herself (the real task of the Warrior). What she was doing certainly wasn't getting her what she wanted. When she re-examined her goals carefully, she saw that her timeline was not realistic. She also admitted to herself that she lacked some of the basic skills and experience necessary to begin a full-time coaching practice. She began to seek out opportunities to acquire those skills and gain more experience and to consider whether or not she wanted to do the groundwork necessary to achieve her goals. Ultimately, she decided to get additional training and enrolled in a more intensive and comprehensive coach-training program. By trusting in Sandra's ability to learn to listen to her own feelings, her coach was able to encourage her to begin to trust in herself; and by encouraging her to set realistic goals and acknowledge her own limits, he was able to help her claim her autonomy.

THE INNER CHILD IN THE WORKPLACE

Unsupervised inner children, or what I like to think of as *inner adolescents*, can be especially troublesome in the workplace when they unconsciously seek parental care and consideration from managers and supervisors or continually challenge the authority of others. Most mature adults have mastered the technical skills they need to do the jobs they are employed to do, but office tensions and disputes seldom involve technical ability or professional know-how. Most workplace problems concern the inability to relate to others in a mature manner and have to do with workers and managers taking things personally instead of professionally. Coaches are often called on to work in this arena.

Andrea's journey. Andrea was so distraught about her work situation that she cried easily, spent lots of time complaining about the manager and company policy, and became a distraction to others in the office. Her manager put her on probation and called on the in-house coach to help with this problem employee. Andrea didn't want to lose her job, and the company, aware of the cost of replacing and training new employees, wanted to keep her. At first Andrea was surprised that she was considered the problem. From her point of view the manager was the one who should be replaced and who needed a coach. She complained, "My boss doesn't understand me; he doesn't want to know how I feel about things. He doesn't know how much pressure I have been under at home. He never cuts me any slack. Others get away with leaving work early and making personal phone calls, but I get reprimands and poor evaluations when I do the same thing. He doesn't like me and doesn't listen to any of the suggestions I have to offer. He needs help with his people skills."

Andrea's inner adolescent was engaged in a power struggle with authority figures in the workplace. She heard every suggestion as criticism, took every statement personally, and, in turn, was contemptuous of all of her boss's actions. When her manager said, "I expect you to be at work on time and to put in 40 clock hours each week," she interpreted this as an indication that the only thing he cared about was the trivia of hours and minutes. She concluded, "He doesn't trust me, doesn't care how I feel, and has no idea of the problems I have in my personal life." Consider how closely this resembles the adolescent's response to the parent who wants him to be home at a reasonable hour and says, "All you care about is having me do what you want, you don't care about my social life, and you don't care that everyone else can stay out later. You only think about yourself, and you don't trust me!"

According to David Whyte, "The workplace carries so much of our desperate need for acknowledgment, for hierarchy, for reward, to be seen, and to be seen as we want to be seen, that we often over-reach ourselves, and our passionate and often violent needs suddenly break through the placid exterior" (Whyte 2001, 125). That is what happened to Andrea.

Like real children, inner children are incapable of self-care and dependent on others to be trustworthy, protect them, and tell them what to do. Therefore, when the Innocent or the Orphan are the only archetypes activated, when we are out of archetypal balance, when we are acting as the inner child, we are blind to our other capabilities. In short, we haven't developed an awareness of ourselves that is independent of the mandates or approval of others. When we don't awaken inner parents, we search forever for someone else—therapist, mate, or boss—to care for us, approve of us, and tell us what to do. And, sadly, even if we find others to do this for us, it's never good enough. In matters of important human relationships, some people remain the eternal child and/or adolescent.

This is why Andrea, bright and accomplished, becomes an adolescent, enraged with her boss yet at the same time wanting him to take care of her. Under other circumstances she is perfectly capable of defending or comforting others, but in significant relationships she has difficulty standing up for, soothing, or nurturing herself. Pearson says, "For most people, the Warrior and the Caregiver are the first adult archetypes to be experienced and integrated into consciousness. Without developing at least one of these, most people emotionally and developmentally remain children" (Pearson 1991, 98).

How to Awaken the Inner Parent

Certainly, many need intensive psychotherapy to work out their parental relationship and learn to care for themselves. However, once coaches truly believe a client has the innate inner resources to develop internal parents and take charge of his or her own life, there are many things they can do to help without immediately classifying clients as disordered or in need of therapy. It isn't always necessary to *teach* clients about archetypes and heroes on a journey; it is only necessary that we *treat* them as heroes on a journey. Coaches who treat clients like the adults they are—showing confidence in their ability to take charge of themselves—foster independence rather than dependence in the clients. (Here I do not dismiss the brutal effects of child abuse and its terrifying consequences, the *wounds* that must be healed before the journey begins. In too many cases, however, psychotherapists, by treating all victims the same, re-victimize their clients by creating a dependency upon the therapist that lasts too long and doesn't allow the client to access innate inner resources.) People need to be given credit for breaking free and taking charge of their own lives, and they must be held accountable when they make a mess of things. Developing inner parents means doing both of these things.

To awaken the archetypal inner parents, we first must examine the developmental tasks of childhood. To become independent of parents, a child must learn trust and autonomy—must learn to trust in the self instead of relying on others. To become independent of parents, children must be able to soothe and to reassure themselves. Also, as children grow they must learn to be autonomous in the sense that they can protect or defend themselves, make goals, set their own limits, *and* at the same time know the extent of their own personal authority.

Once we embrace this theoretical concept, many ways are available to us to help clients grow up and accomplish these essential developmental tasks. Especially helpful is bringing the consciousness of clients into the present moment by treating them as competent adults (which is what good coaches do) and asking them to identify their needs and goals in the working situation. By taking their concerns seriously, and not giving advice or telling them how to behave, we help direct them to resources within themselves.

Andrea's journey continued. Andrea's coach listened to her complaints, then asked her to describe how she wanted to interact with her manager and others in the office. Andrea's attitude began to change when the coach suggested that

she write a detailed description of her own job and of her manager's job. Coach and client worked together to describe her ideal working situation and identify what she would have to do to make this happen. When Andrea examined the job descriptions, she saw that she was asking her manager to take on a parental role. She realized that it wasn't his job to trust her or to show her favoritism, and it wasn't her job to point out what he was doing wrong. She recognized that she needed feedback about job performance, positive and negative, and wanted to know that her manager had, at least, heard her suggestions. (The coach also worked independently with the manager on his management style and ways that he could reach his professional goals and improve employee retention.)

In the long run, however, Andrea saw changes she could make whether the manager made the changes she wanted or not. After some practice and focus on her own goals, she began to alter the way she related to her boss and allowed herself to listen to his criticisms and suggestions without argument. She learned to acknowledge his point of view by listening to and repeating his suggestions even when she thought his criticism unjust.

Now, when Andrea believes she is being unfairly criticized because she has a different sales strategy from her boss, she can hear the criticism, take the feedback, acknowledge it, and move on. With a strong Warrior in place she no longer considers this a personal insult. Importantly, she can differentiate between a difference of opinion and mis-statements of fact. If she is wrongfully accused in a matter of fact, she can stand up for herself and present her requests in a professional way. At work she reminds herself to stick to facts instead of feelings, to ask for what she wants, and to articulate her concerns in a professional rather than a personal manner. And, even though she would like emotional support from her boss, she now seeks that support outside of the office.

BALANCING THE ARCHETYPES AND THE DEVELOPMENTAL TASKS OF THE EGO

Once the archetypes of the Ego are in balance, we realize that we can make our way in the world. We can give up the search for perfect parents and stop blaming others for our shortcomings. We know that if we want the universe to take care of us we will have to play our part. We can then begin the journey to the Soul to discover what that part will be. Awakening the archetypes of the Ego prepares us to begin the journey of individualization—"a process Jung conceived of as a series of initiatory ordeals and transitions we make at various crossroads of our lives" (Levoy 1997, 147).

Although the developmental tasks I relate to the Ego and the Soul correspond in Erikson's model to the life stages of childhood, adolescence, and early adulthood, we encounter these archetypes repeatedly as we spiral through the many cycles of renewal during our lives. If we are fully conscious and aware, each time we return to square one we encounter the archetypes on a deeper level.

Balancing the Masculine and the Feminine

The Caregiver and the Warrior archetypes can also represent internal balance between the masculine and feminine elements of the personality. As the outward role definition of male and female becomes more diverse, we shouldn't confuse women in traditional male roles and men in traditional feminine roles with the true inner androgyny necessary for wholeness. Androgyny is a deeper concern.

The journey is usually different for men than it is for women. Men may have no trouble activating the Warrior archetype, while women may need to work harder to find their own voices and stake their claims in the world. Men, again in general, may have difficulty awakening the Caregiver to soothe the Orphan. What we seek on the journey is a blending, an androgyny that allows each of us to embrace and appreciate all of the masculine and feminine qualities and experience all of the archetypes on the deepest of levels.

Robert Johnson talks about this in terms of the concept of feminine heroism—a quality appropriate for both men and women in today's world.

"Feminine heroism is what is required of us now, of all of us men and women. In the divisive strengths of masculinized world culture, we must hold to the basic simplicities that bind us and make us whole. This is now the Great Quest. No longer can we be the conquering (masculine) hero, who defends his territory, his principles, his woman, his rights. We must become the embracing hero, who finds the right place for each relationship in life, who nurtures and protects and comforts so that growth can take place, not in a field of illusions, but in a field of love and wholeness.

This heroism requires all the skill and intelligence, all the strength and courage, of the heroism with which we are more familiar. Perhaps it requires even more." (Johnson 1991, 95–96)

chapter 1 workbook

ego archetypes

BALANCING THE EGO ARCHETYPES AND PREPARING FOR THE JOURNEY

THE QUESTIONS AND EXERCISES that follow are a compilation of exercises drawn from many sources. Because they relate to Carol S. Pearson's work, many have been inspired by, suggested by, or adapted from her workshops and trainings. Several come from the extensive writings of various coach training institutions and others from the work of Bill O'Hanlon, the brief psychotherapy movement, narrative therapy, and the field of cognitive-behavioral therapy. In addition, many come from my experience as a coach, teacher, and psychotherapist and from my book, *Finding Your Own True North*. Because others and I have modified these so often, it is impossible to document the origin of each question or exercise.

A TRAVEL JOURNAL AND A TIMELINE
If you choose to record these exercises, you will have a record of a very personal map of the journey that you can refer to and add to as your journey continues. I recommend that you select a loose-leaf notebook in which to keep the records of your responses to the exercises. You can also record the observations and conclusions you draw from these responses. Divide your notebook into sections for each archetype and element of the journey with headings such as Call/Fall, Dragons, Calling, Purpose, Ego, Soul, and Self. In addition, space is provided in each workbook for you to make notes as you go along.

Where Have You Come From?
The first section of your notebook can contain a simple timeline. On the left half of the timeline, record the significant events of your *adult* life so far. We don't want to dwell on the past, but we do want to learn from it. Before we embark on a new journey it is important to know where we have been. Some roads don't need to be traveled more than once, but others can be enjoyed over and over again.

Once you have found yourself, however, you will want to decide on a destination, so leave room on the right half of the line for events to come. Determine how long you think you might live.

Place that date toward the right side of the line, but leave room after it for goals that go beyond your life span. Right now just fill in the events leading up to today.

Where Are You Now in Terms of Your Archetypal Awareness?

Before continuing with your timeline, take the *Pearson-Marr Archetype Indicator*® instrument online available at www.capt.org. With the results in hand you will have a graphic representation of where you are in terms of archetypal awareness at this point in your life.

Where Do You Want to Go and What Do You Want to Do When You Get There?

After you have reached your present age on the timeline, extend the line into the future for as many years as you expect to live. Place on the line your goals for the next five, ten, fifteen, and twenty years. At this point pencil in your goals. Also take some time to list things about yourself and the way that you have lived your life that you hope will exceed your life span. We will return to this again during the self-coaching process.

EXERCISES FOR THE EGO ARCHETYPES

We call on the Ego archetypes through movement and experience, tuning in to all of our senses to activate these energies. We feel these archetypes in our bodies and can awaken them by assuming certain facial expressions and bodily positions. In the following exercises, hold each of the following positions until you experience the archetype.

First, find a quiet place and take several minutes to allow yourself to call forth each of the following archetypes. Savor the experience of each archetype as you work through each exercise. Then answer the questions in writing in your own personal journey log. These responses are for you alone, or to share with your coach or guide. Later you may want to share these with others, but I suggest that you hold off until you have taken the journey and returned.

Calling on the Innocent

We experience the Innocent when we feel loved and the world seems a safe place. Open your eyes wide, throw back your arms, and bask in the good warm light of the morning sun or the imagined smile of a loved one. Think of a time when someone's eyes lit up each time you entered the room and remember how it felt to experience warmth, love, safety, and trust. If you have never experienced this with another person, recall the complete acceptance and love of a dog or another pet or even a stuffed animal. Remember Radar O'Reilly on the television program *Mash* and his beloved Teddy Bear?

When you have fully engaged and experienced the Innocent, ask the archetype to write you a letter to let you know what she wants or needs from you, or what she can do for you. Use the space provided here or write the letter in your notebook.

For example: Dorothy, a competent woman in her mid-sixties with three grown children and a successful career, was surprised to hear her Innocent say, "I am your Innocent and you keep me locked up most of the time. Don't you trust me? Are you afraid that people will think you are naïve or some sort of Pollyanna if you look on the bright side or make mistakes? You can give love with no expectation of return; it will not cost you anything. You need me now more than ever; innocence isn't just for the young."

_____

_____

_____

_____

_____

_____

_____

_____

_____

_____

_____

_____

_____

_____

_____

Notice your response to your Innocent. Were you surprised or did you expect the response you received? Write your responses in here or in your notebook.

_____

_____

_____

_____

_____

_____

_____

_____

_____

_____

Calling on the Orphan

We experience the unbalanced Orphan when the world is a hostile place. Slump in a chair with shoulders hunched, study the floor as if you were memorizing the pattern on the rug. Cringe. Imagine what it would be like if no one ever noticed when you entered the room or if you feared at all times for your safety. Try to be invisible. Stay in this position until you feel it throughout your body. Now, write yourself a letter from the Orphan.

For example: The same woman wrote, "I am your Orphan and I am pissed. Over and over again you tell me to shut up. You pretend you can't hear me, or that I haven't any right to exist, and you think you are supposed to have it all together and not have the same needs that other people have. You think you're not supposed to feel scared or inadequate; you even seem to think you aren't supposed to feel. You try to hide your disappointments. I need somebody to take care of me. There is more than one form of neglect and abandonment."

_____

_____

_____

_____

_____

_____

_____

_____

_____

_____

_____

_____

_____

_____

_____

_____

_____

_____

_____

_____

Notice your response to the Orphan. Does she call forth the Caregiver or the Warrior in you? Is it all right for you to have these feelings and not do anything about them? Write your responses in your notebook.

_____

_____

_____

_____

_____

_____

_____

_____

_____

Calling on the Caregiver

We experience the Caregiver when we nurture ourselves. Embrace yourself and gently rock back and forth. Feel the warmth and acceptance of sheltering arms. Again, stay in this position until you can feel what it is like to be taken care of but not smothered. You are in charge of wrapping sheltering arms around yourself and of taking them away when you no longer need them. Once you have fully experienced the Caregiver archetype, call on it to write another letter.

For example: Dorothy's Caregiver wrote, "I am almost too tired to write because I've been doing all the work in this department for years and years. I need some help. You have me taking care of everyone's feelings but your own. I'm the one who has to make everybody happy, smooth over all the arguments, watch what you say, and never, ever make anyone angry or sad. God forbid anyone else should think that you were selfish or inconsiderate! And the kids, do you really think they must never have any disappointments or sadness in their lives and you have to make everything better? Who told you that you had to be the mother of the year? I think you are in the running for the martyr of the year. Let me take care of you for a change."

_____

_____

_____

_____

_____

_____

_____

_____

_____

_____

_____

_____

_____

_____

_____

_____

_____

_____

_____

_____

_____

_____

What was your response to the Caregiver? Whatever it was, it was your response. There are no wrong responses. Write your responses in your notebook.

_____

_____

_____

_____

_____

_____

_____

_____

_____

_____

_____

_____

Calling on the Warrior

To experience the Warrior, stand tall. Hold your arms outstretched in front of you parallel to the floor with palms facing outward. Say "no" in a firm voice. Feel your sense of authority throughout your body and in your voice. Now, assume the same position and say "yes" in a firm voice. In this instance you are saying yes to the self, an essential component of the hero's journey. Once you have fully called for the Warrior, write another letter.

For example: Dorothy's Warrior wrote, "Well, it's about time. I have so many things I want to do and have been waiting for you to get around to me. I have some plans for our future and some limits I want to set on how you have been beating yourself up over your inability to make your children happy and trying to please everybody in the universe. I know exactly what you want to do and what you don't want to do. I've seen you letting other people take advantage of you. Now I'm going to show you how to stand up for yourself without knocking someone else down. However, you are going to tell the Caregiver that she will have to face the fact that other people won't always like it and won't always agree and understand. It's all right for others to be angry. Once I teach you how to handle your own anger, you'll be able to let other people have theirs. And, another thing: how come you call on me with some people and not others? I notice that you use me a lot at work but not at home or with your kids."

_____

_____

_____

_____

_____

_____

_____

_____

_____

_____

_____

_____

_____

_____

_____

_____

_____

_____

What were your responses to your Warrior? Write your responses in your notebook.

_____

_____

_____

_____

_____

_____

_____

_____

_____

OTHER EGO EXERCISES

In addition to these exercises, you can take many everyday actions to bring the needed archetype into your awareness. To evoke the Warrior, you can change your posture (think how differently you can assert yourself when you are sitting or standing tall). You can manage your time, set your limits by telling others what you will and won't do, and differentiate between negotiable situations and arguments. You can evoke the Caregiver by making a tape of soothing self-talk, listening to music or poetry that reassures you, remembering times when you coped well with difficult situations, and consciously caring for yourself by eating properly, exercising, or getting enough sleep.

Awakening and balancing the archetypes is an intentional act. Think of five other things you can do to awaken your Caregiver and Warrior. Write them down.

_____

_____

_____

_____

_____

Look back over each of the letters you wrote from the archetypes. Do you see a theme? Think of something that symbolizes each archetype. Use drawings, photos, or found objects to symbolize the archetypes. One client chose a statue of a mother and child to keep her Caregiver in mind, and for years I kept a ceramic breastplate of a woman warrior in my office to remind me to keep my Warrior active. Many people use rainbows to remind them of their Innocent, and one client uses newspaper photos of war victims to recall his Orphan. Remember, to awaken these archetypes we have to take action or deliberately and consciously decide not to take action rather than acting from a default position (unconsciously).

BALANCING THE EGO ARCHETYPES

Now that you know how to awaken the archetypes, the next step is to learn when to call on the archetypes. Archetypal balance is a matter of knowing which archetype to call on in any given situation. Like riding a bicycle, once you get the hang of it balancing the archetypes will become automatic; but at first it needs to be intentional and very conscious. Initially, you may be unaware of being out of balance because you have always responded or reacted in a certain way. Begin with some self-observation exercises.

Self-Observation

At the end of each day review your interactions with yourself and with others to see whether or not you have balanced your archetypes. Finish the following sentences.

I told myself not to feel angry, sad, scared, lonely when . . .

_____

_____

_____

I allowed myself to feel angry, sad, scared, happy, lonely, confused by . . .

_____

_____

_____

I allowed someone else to cross my personal boundaries when I . . .

_____

_____

_____

I set firm limits and expressed myself clearly when I . . .

_____

_____

_____

I soothed myself with self-talk and encouragement by . . .

_____

_____

_____

I upset myself with negative self-talk and self-criticism when I . . .

_____

_____

_____

I asked for help when . . .

_____

_____

_____

I could have asked for help but didn't when . . .

_____

_____

_____

I kept myself from asking for help by . . .

_____

_____

_____

I allowed other people to "hurt my feelings" when . . .

_____

_____

_____

Other Questions to Ask the Self

Here are some further questions to ask the Self that will help in balancing your archetypes. Reflect on all of these questions. Write about them in your workbook.

How do I know when to trust myself? What is an example of trusting or not trusting myself? What happens to me when I don't trust myself?

_____

_____

_____

_____

When was the last time I experienced a sense of orphaning or abandonment or rejection? What was my reaction to that experience? When I sense the Orphan in others, how do I respond?

_____

_____

_____

_____

_____

_____

How do I acknowledge my own aloneness, vulnerability, and misgivings? If I were to call on someone else for help and support, whom would I call upon? What, specifically, would I ask of someone else? What would I do if I asked for help and didn't get it? In what areas of my life do I feel vulnerable?

_____

_____

_____

_____

_____

_____

How can I receive support as well as give it? Give examples. How do I respond when others offer help?

_____

_____

_____

_____

_____

_____

How can I take feedback without viewing it as criticism? When was the last time I felt criticized? How could I have called on a Warrior or a Caregiver to help me sort out my response? How can I accept disappointment and failure without blaming others?

_____

_____

_____

_____

_____

_____

Am I aware of my own emotional needs, and do I understand that others do not have to take care of those needs? What exactly are my emotional needs, and how do I expect others to tend to them?

_____
_____
_____
_____
_____
_____
_____
_____
_____
_____
_____
_____
_____
_____
_____
_____
_____
_____

Chapter Two

TAKING THE SOUL JOURNEY: FINDING YOUR CENTER

THE ARCHETYPES OF THE SOUL			
The Seeker	The Destroyer	The Lover	The Creator

"Our work is to make ourselves visible in the world. This is the soul's individual journey, and the soul would rather fail at its own life than succeed at someone else's."

— DAVID WHYTE,
*Crossing the Unknown Sea:
Work as a Pilgrimage of Identity*

"The soul is the dark and earthy soil where we can cultivate the higher power within us. We get to know our soul by exploring our dreams, fantasies and imagination, territories where nothing is forbidden."
— SHELDON KOPP,
If You Meet the Buddha on the Road, Kill Him! The Pilgrimage of Psychotherapy Patients

THE DEVELOPMENTAL TASK of the Soul Journey is the establishment of a separate identity, which in turn enables us to be intimate with others.

The completion of the developmental tasks of the Ego, the Preparation phase of the Journey, has a similar impact on all humans. We prepare for the Journey by learning how to take care of ourselves; interact in socially appropriate ways; feed, clothe, and protect ourselves; modulate our emotions; and care for our bodily functions—the Ego is concerned with a shared reality. Once we have learned how and when to call on the archetypes of the Ego, we are ready for any number of soul journeys where we may plunge into the existential, the abstract, the inner world of the imagination, the unconscious, and the surreal. Each of us experiences and emerges from this part of the Journey in a different way.

On the Soul Journey we are concerned not so much with actual life, death, and survival as we are with the *meaning* of life and death. Where the language of the Ego is essentially a universally understood language of the body/mind, the language of the soul is myth, symbol, song, art, literature, poetry, and ritual. This language is interpreted differently by each of us as we take our separate paths to the developmental task of discovering our identities.

Soul means different things to different people.[1] I use the term in the poetic rather than the religious sense. Gregg Levoy calls soul the place of the "deeper brain—intuition, feeling, sensing, instinct, dream" (Levoy 1997, 20). Poet David Whyte says that soul is "measured by vitality, by depth of feeling and depth of thought. But most of all, it is measured by the experience of participation" (Whyte 1994). Consider soul in this context as an abstraction to be experienced rather than defined: a metaphor for Jung's concept of the soul as "an autonomous personality that structures our inner life, and is projected out into the world" (Robertson 1992). Considering the nature of these descriptions, it is no surprise, then, that the Soul archetypes are more difficult to personify or picture than are the Ego archetypes. They are awakened by different means.

THE NATURE OF THE SOUL JOURNEY

The pace of the journey slows as we enter the realm of the Soul. Although awareness of the Ego archetypes is close to the surface and the archetypes are easily summoned by our interactions with others, the archetypes of the Soul are deeper and more personal. We need time to reflect, go deep inside, listen to the interior voices, feel yearnings and longings, and allow our passions to emerge. The soul is concerned with deep desires that we have often hidden from ourselves in the mistaken belief that all desires are somehow forbidden.

On his map of life chapters and transitions—the cycle of continuous renewal—Frederic Hudson names one of life's transitions the "cocoon." He suggests that when we have finished with one difficult chapter of life we should enter a cocoon, a period of reflection where we withdraw from life, examine what we really want, and discover who we really are (Hudson and McLean 1996).

Each person, however, must structure a cocoon or a Soul Journey to fit unique needs. As you begin the Soul Journey, you may not be able to withdraw completely into a cocoon, but you can structure time and create spaces in which to turn inward, listen, and reflect.

In addition, soul work is solo work. A cocoon only has room for one person. Although you can use the guidance of a coach or guide, you do not need their approval. Soul work is not a matter to be discussed with or approved by others in your social circle. That is, the things you write and what you learn about yourself are for you alone. No one else has to understand them or agree with them. You are finding your own identity, not comparing yourself to others or telling anyone else how to find her or his identity. You must critique and evaluate and savor your own experiences and actions, not those of anyone else.

THE LANGUAGE OF THE SOUL

Taking the Journey and Depth Coaching require us to learn the language of the Soul. The Ego speaks in the common language of our basic emotions and the sensible language of rational thought. My Ego and your Ego can converse. The Soul (like the unconscious), however, speaks in symbol and metaphor, dreams, images, and poetry.

You enter the realm of the soul when you take the time to meditate, learn yoga, the *relaxation response*, centering prayer, or when you study the ageless myths.

Discover the pathways and practices that fit for you. Make the time and find a place to fit them into your life. Read aloud the poetry of contemporary poets David Whyte or Mary Oliver, savor the classic poems of Rainer Maria Rilke, and experience the beauty and wisdom of Rumi. Use tapes as guides to meditation. Listen to music that stirs your soul.

Pay attention to your day dreams and night dreams but remember, dreams and the unconscious speak to us symbolically, not literally. For example, in the language of the soul, thoughts and dreams of death may be telling you that something has to end, be cut out, to die, so that something else can be born. Be careful, however, only the dreamer can interpret each symbol and each dream. Coaches and therapists can help you interpret a dream but only *you* will know when an interpretation fits your personal unconscious. Beware of those who tell you what your dreams mean. That is not the function of a coach. I have found Robert Johnson's *Inner Work: Using Dreams and Active Imagination for Personal Growth* (1986 Harper and Row) an excellent resource for clients to use for dream interpretation and other forms of inner work with Soul archetypes.

THE COACHING QUESTION

Having talked about the soul language as in terms of myth, symbol, and poetry, it may seem strange that I add a discussion of the coaching question. We usually think of question and answer as an intellectual activity unsuited to the soul. However, there are certain questions that lead us inward—toward the heart rather than the head—and form an integral part of any coaching experience. Questions such as form the heart of the coaching conversation: What do you seek? What do you desire? What makes this so scary for you? What would it be like to do something you loved passionately? What do you need to create to make that happen? Here we meet the unique notion of the coaching question: a question that is meant to create an experience or evoke an action within the person being questioned; a question designed to lead the client inward; a question whose answer is significant *only* to the person being asked the question. Because these powerful questions and inquiries are directed to inner experience they cannot always be answered immediately and the answers will be different for each person (which is why entering a cocoon, or taking time to isolate yourself from the world, is such a powerful exercise). Even those who hire a coach with a specific performance goal in mind often find that they want to slow down and take the time to take this inner journey (both in session and in coaching assignments for work between sessions) to help guide them to their special paths.

We can begin now to call forth the archetypes of the Soul with questions and imagery.

"The quest always begins with yearning. We feel discontented, confined, alienated, or empty. Often we do not even have a name for what is missing, but we long for that mysterious something."

— CAROL S. PEARSON,
Awakening the Heroes Within

The seeker makes its presence known through restlessness. We are aware that we are looking for something, and yet not quite sure what that something is. The presence of this archetype signifies the beginning of the journey and may come to us in the form of a *call* or a *fall*.

A Call or a Fall

". . . no matter what stage or grade of life, the call brings up the curtain. The familiar life horizon has been outgrown; the old concepts, ideals and emotional patterns no longer fit; the time for the passing of a threshold is at hand."

— JOSEPH CAMPBELL,
The Hero with a Thousand Faces

"Calling becomes a calling to life, rather than imagined in conflict with life. Calling to honesty rather than to success, to caring and mating, to service and struggle for the sake of living. This view offers a revision of vocation . . . it offers another idea of calling altogether, in which life is the work."

— JAMES HILLMAN,
Re-Visioning Psychology

> *"Calling is active. It's a summons to play our part. Calling is a present moment notion; it is actively alive, tugging on us during our entire lifetime."*
> — J. Leider and D. A. Shapiro
> *Whistle While You Work: Heeding Your Life's Calling*

Some journeys begin with the call. The call is something you feel you *must* do—a journey you feel compelled to take. Some view the call as sacred—a call from God or the gods to follow a particular vocation or share a particular gift. We don't need to decide here whether the call is secular or sacred, but we do need to be certain that a call is coming from inside ourselves and not from the expectations of others. However, we often have difficulty hearing a call when the language of the heart is so different from the language of the head, and the words in the head— the interjected voices of others—are loud and well articulated. Once you are conversant with your own calls and callings and familiar with the voices of your heart, you will be able to help others hear theirs.

Not all journeys begin with a call; some journeys begin with a fall. Depression, despair, and anxiety following a stressful, traumatic, or unfulfilling experience can be a call to turn inward and examine the way we have been living our lives, rather than symptoms of psychological disorders.[2] After all, Adam and Eve didn't hear a call to go forth from the garden and start a new life. They suffered a fall from innocence and were involuntarily cast into the real world. While in a trance-like state of innocence and dependency, the lives of Adam and Eve had no meaning. On the Journey we wake up from parental and societal trances and make an *intentional* transition from one stage of life to another.

Some of the most dramatic journeys begin with a wound (or betrayal): a spouse who walks out, a disabling accident, a layoff from a once-secure job, or a diagnosis of a life-threatening illness. All of these events can give you the opportunity to re-examine your life and can call you to the journey rather than sink you into despair.

Be aware, also, that a fall, or a call, is not always dramatic. The fall—the awakening to reality, the realization that you have been climbing a ladder against the wrong wall or counting on others for security that can come only from within—can also be experienced as a vague feeling of discontent or apathy. What is important is that these feelings must be experienced, not medicated, sedated, or therapied away. Within that experience we can often hear the call. The Journey begins as we allow ourselves to pay attention to and acknowledge these experiences and emotions.

You know the Seeker is calling when you feel alienated, dissatisfied, empty, *or* when you sense a new opportunity knocking and want things to be better than they are. You can hear the Seeker when you hear an inner voice telling you that your life could be different or that *you* can make a difference in your family, your company, or in the world. Seeking often has to do with the search for meaning. It is a spiritual quest more than a psychological or practical one. The question, What do I seek? is not always easy to answer. Initially we can only allow the question itself to be the invitation to the quest. Wanting something better and uneasiness with the way things are signify a call. Being willing to acknowledge that uneasiness can be the beginning of a journey.

Answering a call or experiencing the Seeker is not a self-improvement project; we are not analyzing what is wrong and trying to fix it. Instead we seek to actualize and use all of the resources available to us. Think of how your response is different when I ask, What are you looking for? or What do you seek? Compare that to your response to the question, What is wrong?

I suspect that when I ask you what you seek, you go *inside* to answer the question and that the answer will be personal, unique, and involve the future. If I ask what is wrong you are more likely to describe a history of a problem, and very often a problem whose solution lies outside of you.

Also, after a lifetime of following somebody else's path, some people may also need to be given permission not to know exactly what they want right now. You don't have to have the answers. In fact, the Soul Journey involves keeping the questions in your consciousness rather than finding the answers. You can sit with the notion of not knowing and experience what some have called the *creative void*. The task of the coach or the guide is to approach people with genuine curiosity—not to judge or evaluate their responses, but merely to acknowledge their present position and introduce them to the language of the soul. The coach asks, What is it that you want? What are you seeking? What do you desire? What would that be like? and leads you deeper and deeper inside yourself.

Don't be discouraged if your calls are not consistently strong. Calls don't start strong and stay strong. In *Callings: Finding and Following an Authentic Life*, Gregg Levoy urges us to stay with the call and not be discouraged by its inevitable waxing and waning. He reminds us that friction and chaos are essential elements of the call. He asks us to think of calls as questions—questions that we don't need to answer outright but will pursue throughout a lifetime (Levoy 1997, 9).

Coaching the Seeker: Calls and Callings

"Each one of us has unique potential—distinct, God given gifts—with which to serve the world. These gifts provide us with a source of identity in the world. But until we connect who we are with what we do, that source remains untapped."

— RICHARD J. LEIDER,
*The Power of Purpose:
Creating Meaning in Your Life and Work*

When we hear a call or begin a quest we might begin to ask, What am I being called to do? However, calls seldom specify a specific job. More often calls come in the form of a compelling need to do a certain thing, or a feeling of being drawn to certain activities such as teaching, healing in some way, understanding the nature of things, or producing something. Only a fortunate few have a specific calling; others feel a call to investigate, to instruct, to help others overcome obstacles, to manage things or people, or to design. Following your call may lead to any number of different occupations and pursuits. Being aware of your calling can even make a present job more meaningful.

Many of us don't recognize a call because we look at things from the outside in (from other people's points of view); we listen to what others tell us we should do and give them undue authority (the power) to discourage or encourage us. Some of us get on the wrong track in seeking a calling by focusing outside ourselves and saying what we want to *be*, not *do*. We say we want to be writers—but we don't write; we want to be actors—but we don't try out for any plays.

Real callings are closely related to what we love to do, or what we feel we must do, not what we want to be. If you find yourself thinking in the "what I want to be" mode, ask yourself what, specifically, it is about this job or profession or course of training that is compelling to you; then look for aspects of this calling that are present in your daily life. Think of what your life would be like if you were doing more of that in your job; then, explore to discover other ways you get those needs met.

Beth's journey. Beth said she wanted to be an actress. I asked her what it would be like for her to be an actress and what she would have in her life as an actress that she didn't have now? After careful examination and thought, she replied that as an actress she would be the center of attention, would have the chance to portray different characters, and would be paid for performing. As she visualized herself doing these things and lived with these images for a while, she realized that she truly loved to perform and that her calling was "to perform to give other people pleasure."

Although she did not immediately give up the idea of acting, she realized that there were other ways she could satisfy her desires. Ultimately, she began to investigate new opportunities to answer her calling to perform, such as a job as a teacher where she could bring to life the characters in the books she would read to her young students.

Positive projection. Although I have asked you to go inside yourselves to find your hidden treasures, there is another way to discover hidden gifts by looking at your projections. Look outward at those you admire and then search for those traits hidden in yourself. Frequently, we project out to other people those qualities we can't recognize in ourselves. We usually consider projection a negative activity—in which we project all of our bad qualities onto other people. There are also positive projections that help us to discover resources, abilities, and good qualities we didn't know we had. These positive projections can direct us to gifts and callings we have previously been unable to appreciate.

Mary's journey. Having spent many years in therapy to heal the wounds of an abusive childhood and escape the domination of her family of origin, Mary, at age 50, was ready to begin the Journey. When her friends and her family urged her to get a job, she sought a coach to help her decide what she wanted to do with the rest of her life. She had a high school education and no job training. Although she had overcome many obstacles in her life, she had a difficult time identifying any personal treasures and gifts. She believed she was far less gifted than others.

When I asked her to think about and write about the people she admired, she named several teachers, counselors, and workshop presenters. When asked exactly what it was that she admired about them, she concluded that she envied their ability to overcome adversity, make a difference in the lives of other people, and help others reach their potential.

Drawing on that awareness I asked her to look at her lifeline and reflect back on her life to see if she could find instances where she had made a difference in the lives of others, whether by example or by some direct act of kindness or compassion. Slowly, over time, she recalled the times she had helped others who were in trouble, and befriended or advocated for those who couldn't speak up for themselves.

Mary began to allow herself to claim some positive shadow qualities (perseverance, curiosity, ability to overcome obstacles, empathy). She added these to the things she already knew about herself (especially her lifelong love of children) and realized that she could combine her gifts in pursuit of a career as an elementary school teacher. With a destination in mind, her focus changed from a desire to conform to social pressure to do something productive to a desire to take a journey to fulfillment.

Remember, too, that seeking or listening to a call doesn't always result in a change in profession or even in making personal changes that enhance your present job. Seeking and hearing a call are concerned also with the call of the unknown, the expansion of consciousness, or breaking the bonds of the ego and the constraints of our society. Seeking begins the process of individuation where we start to discover who we truly are and find the meaning of our lives—not the meaning of life—but *the meaning of our own lives and our place in the scheme of things.* Seeking begins the journey, but seeking is continuous, active, and never satisfied—a beginning and a continuing, not an end.

Each of the Soul archetypes calls forth another, and once awakened these archetypes stay present in our awareness and available whenever we need them. Answering the call of the Seeker begins an intentional transition to a new phase of life, but at the soul level this isn't necessarily connected to achievement or accomplishment. Pearson says that for a real transformation to take place we need to "die to our former selves." We must call on the Destroyer, face the dragons, and rid ourselves of those things that impede the journey and prevent our development as individuals.

THE DESTROYER ARCHETYPE

The part that enables us to rid ourselves of things that no longer add value to our lives.

GIFTS
Humility and acceptance.

ASK YOURSELF . . .
What outmoded or borrowed ideas or dreams do I need to let go of? What is keeping me from living the life I want? Can I face the idea of my own mortality and help others to face theirs?

"Whether we believe in an afterlife or not, until we stop denying the reality of death, it will inevitably possess us."

— CAROL S. PEARSON,
Awakening the Heroes Within

The Seeker came forth in your yearnings and desires, as you heard the call and began the quest. Opening yourself up to the awareness of hidden desires and going forth to find the treasures can be pleasant, stimulating, and exciting. Calling forth the Destroyer, however, is not always so pleasant a task. Inevitably, for each path taken, another path is not. You may have to let go of old habits, old friends, hopes of security, and some of your dreams. You experience the Destroyer when you feel pain, suffering, tragedy, loss, *and* also when you experience the liberation of letting go.

Dragons

"The need to take the journey is innate in the species. If we do not risk, if we play prescribed social roles instead of taking our journeys, we feel numb; we experience a sense of alienation, a void, and emptiness inside. People who are discouraged from slaying dragons internalize the urge and slay themselves by declaring war on their fat, their selfishness, or some other attribute they think does not please."
— CAROL S. PEARSON,
The Hero Within: Six Archetypes We Live By

Having heard the call or faced the call that begins the journey, we soon come face to face with obstacles that can force us to turn back before we even begin to find the treasures of our true selves. As you asked yourself the calling questions, were you aware of nagging voices telling you that you couldn't do what you might want to do, that it would cost too much, or that it was selfish to want certain things? Some people never allow themselves to want anything because they cannot bear the thought of not getting what they want; those people are not ready for the journey.

The Hudson Institute calls the obstacles to the journey *boulders*,[3] and Coaches Training Institute and others call them *gremlins*.[4] In the language of the journey they are dragons. As we begin the Soul Journey, we first ask the Destroyer to help us face the dragons.

Nietzsche described the dragon as a monster covered with scales on which were written the words "thou shalt." Joseph Campbell adds, ". . . some [thou shalts or shall nots] are

prohibitions from four thousand years ago; others from this morning's headlines" (Campbell and Moyers 1988, 154). The world is full of dragons who are sometimes very difficult to distinguish from your own thoughts. You may only become aware of them when you hear an inner voice saying "you should" or "you can't," or find that you have a hard time admitting that you don't know something or can't say "I was wrong." Although it seems that dragons lurk in the forests all around us and the road is littered with boulders, we are often surprised to realize that both dragons and boulders, like the Wicked Witch of the West, melt when doused with the cold water of reality and confronted by the authentic voice of the self.

Battles with dragons of other peoples' expectations require careful strategy, because other peoples' expectations slip into our thoughts without our realizing it, and we confuse these inner voices with our own. Most often we can recognize these voices as belonging to specific others such a mother who said, "You should" or "You can't" or "You'd better not," or a father who asked imperiously, "Who do you think you are?" The dragon voice may once have had a purpose but is now outdated. It could be the voice that warned you not to make your father angry when you were ten years old. This voice has turned into the inner critic who tells you that you aren't good enough, resists change, and keeps you in a rut.

We fight the battle with the dragon inside ourselves, where instead of challenging or succumbing to the authority of others we awaken our internal authority (in the language of our Warrior archetype) and say out loud, "I will," "I can," or "I won't." Notice you don't necessarily have to slay the dragon by confronting abusive parents, bosses, or friends. You can simply speak for yourself, announce your intentions, and follow through with your own actions.

Different archetypes respond to dragons in different ways, and we are apt to respond differently at different times in our lives. The young often respond by believing dragons to be outside and say, "I can't do that because they won't let me." When we are very young that is certainly true, but often I hear clients say, "I could never do that because my wife (husband, boss, mother, father) would have a fit" or "My husband would explode if I told him I wanted to go back to school." Or, "I told him I was angry but it didn't work." Although there are external obstacles, more often, it is not other people but the dragon inside who is in charge of our behavior.

What is keeping you from getting what you want? What is standing in your way? Ask yourself how you prevent yourself from getting what you want. Is the obstacle really out there, or is it inside? We all have interior voices that speak to us and keep us imprisoned in the jails they built for us. Many have the voice that says, "Who do you think you are?" Others the one that says, "What will people think?"[5]

─────────────

Eileen's journey. Eileen had a voice that told her that she should always think of others before she thought of herself. She wanted to begin a course of study that would lead to a new career and take her away from home for several weeks at a time. She felt that her husband was standing in her way because she knew it would inconvenience him and upset their routine if she were away for several weeks at a time. Inwardly, she blamed him for having to give up this opportunity. Her coach asked: "What would you need to do to create this opportunity for yourself? What requests would you need to make? What actions could you take? What arrangements can you make?"

Eileen was surprised to realize that she had not even spoken out loud about her interest in the course. Her dragon had told her that it would be inconsiderate of her and kept her from speaking her own desires. When she spoke from her own heart and said what she wanted to do, she was amazed to find that her husband respected her desire. Her only roadblock was one she created for herself.

A writer's journey. A writer had an imperial voice that told her that her work was no good and that she hadn't any right to voice her opinions. As long as she thought of this voice as a residue of years of criticism from her mother, she believed that she would have to work on the problem in psychotherapy or confront her mother in person. When

she realized that this was a boulder or a dragon that would remain with her long after her mother was gone, she accepted it as a part of herself and took charge of her own mind. She tamed her dragon and allowed it to speak only when she was on the final draft and only then when she needed a copy editor.

─────────────

It is easy to see, therefore, that the biggest boulders and dragons are the interjected and embodied expectations of family, friends, or society. These are quite clear because they speak in plain words, saying, "You should have accomplished more by this time," or "What is the matter with you?" or "Why can't you be like other people?" Even now, as I write I hear a voice in my head that says, "Why haven't you made more progress than this? You have been at this for too long. Why are you having so much trouble with the introduction to this book?" Do those voices help me or spur me on? No, they distract and discourage. I have finally learned that it is useless to confront or argue with them or answer their "why" questions. Instead I look for ways to replace their voices or use them in a different way. I find it more useful to keep my eyes on the goal and focus on what I am trying to do rather than why I am not doing it.

We each need to find ways to talk to dragon voices and turn them into something helpful. We can call on the Destroyer to eliminate these useless distractions that diminish our lives, keep us prisoners of the past, and hide our gifts and treasures.

─────────────

Claire's journey. Claire's dragon of perfectionism held her marriage to such a high standard it looked like the relationship would not survive. She rated her marriage a two on a scale of one to ten, and the ten she described was truly "a marriage made in heaven." When facing the dragon of her perfectionism, she held a conversation with the dragon in which she agreed to keep it on part-time by redefining perfection (the dragon's role) and facing the fact that the only part of the relationship completely in her control was her own behavior. She examined the way she reacted to her spouse. She saw the many ways in which she tried to change his behavior or take care of his feelings and agreed to a one-week trial where she would behave as a *ten* no matter how he responded. After a week she decided that she would have to throw out the whole idea of a rating scale and perfectionism in her marriage. She put the dragon to work in the area of her skills as a fine seamstress where she could attain and maintain high standards without involving anyone else.

The dragon of perfectionism often coerces us into believing that others must be perfect, too, and we believe it is our job to hold others to our standards. People rationalize their high expectations for others by proclaiming that they hold themselves to high standards as well. Claire was surprised to find that when she stopped evaluating her husband and concentrated on herself the relationship improved dramatically.

Remember, too, that the Destroyer, like other aspects of the unconscious, speaks to us in symbol and metaphor.

Karen's journey. After being asked to consider the question, What do you need to change to live the life of your desires? Karen noticed that images of knives appeared in her dreams, daydreams, and drawings. She was frightened for fear that it meant that she was going to hurt herself or someone else. After checking out her previous behavior and her psychological history (and for the time being asking her to lock away the knives in her house), I asked her to consider the many meanings these knives might have to her. After meditating, drawing, and writing in her journal, she concluded that she needed to cut the umbilical cord and stop relying on her mother as a lifeline. She did not need to cut off the relationship completely but did need to change it. She also saw that she needed to carve out a niche for herself in her profession in which she was in competition with her mother. The knives were symbols of needed change that ultimately led her to call on several archetypes to help her claim her identity and find her own place in the world.

Karen's dragon was the internalized voice of her mother who criticized and belittled her. She did not have to slay her dragon by confronting or cutting off all contact with her mother. Nor did she need to explain the situation to her mother. Mother did not have to understand, Karen did. She had to

assert herself, speak with her own voice, follow her own bliss, and allow her mother to deal with her own dragons.

———————

Once we realize that the dragon is a part of us, and not an external force, we are completely in charge of the way we respond to it. We can't slay dragons by telling ourselves not to pay attention to them or turning on ourselves and condemning ourselves for allowing them to run our lives. When we become aware of a dragon and recognize it for what it is, we can choose our actions accordingly.

"And so, when the dragon is thoroughly dead, with all its 'thou shalts' overcome, the lion [that is, the person loaded down with injunctions and rules] is transformed into a child moving out of its own nature, like a wheel impelled from its own hub. No more rules to obey. No more rules derived from the historical needs and tasks of the local society, but the pure impulse to living of a life in flower." (Campbell and Moyers 1988, 54)

Coaching the Destroyer

Many coaches ask people to eliminate energy drainers in their lives—a cluttered desk, a to-do list that is ten pages long, a garage or attic filled with toys belonging to children who now have children of their own. This, of course, is a marvelous idea. Coaches will work with clients to list their specific energy drainers and then help them to find ways to eliminate drainers to make room for other activities, passions, and people. However, there are times when we have to go deeper and face the dragon that created the problem in the first place. Often when clients seem to be stuck, or when you find yourself stuck, dragons are at work.

———————

Don and Nancy's journey. Don listed his energy drainers as a cluttered desk and a to-do list that he never finished. Working with time and space management systems and learning to delegate worked well for him and gave him time and space for the important things in his life.

However, as hard as she tried, Nancy, who was unemployed and searching for a job, couldn't follow through on a system of eliminating her energy drainers. Unlike Don, her difficulty was deeper. No outside advice on space management could compete with the interior voices that told her that she could have found a job long ago if she really wanted one, that she was lazy and her inability to clean up the clutter proved it. Dialogues with the dragons revealed to her that she was evaluating herself by outmoded standards and rebelling against parents who were no longer alive. Nancy's dragons kept her from discovering her true treasures (talents), which lay in a creative field, not the one where she sought employment based on her past experience and training. Balancing activities and external demands is no substitute for inner harmony and finding your own path.

A coach's journey. A talented coach in training was reluctant to begin working as a coach. In an exercise on "listening to the self" she heard an ancient dragon-like voice, somehow connected to her early religious training. It chanted to her that she was not worthy to take on such a heavy responsibility. Without deep dragon work, no amount of marketing information, cheerleading, or additional training could have helped her to go on to a successful career.

———————

Other Uses of the Destroyer

The Destroyer helps us to see where we are on the longitudinal journey through life. If we don't face our mortality, we can't truly assign meaning to our lives, play our parts, and use our gifts. Leider asks us to face our fears about death and to look back over each phase of life to identify the core questions in each one (Leider 1997). If we fail to do this, our friendships and relationships will be less meaningful, for we will act as if we had all the time in the world to mend fences and to acknowledge and express our love and devotion.

To many people the word "Destroyer" has a negative connotation, but remember that all of nature and all living systems require a cleaning out; death and decay are essential parts of life. The Destroyer can also be thought of as a remover, an eliminator, or a culler. Picture your house or apartment if you never cleaned or culled out useless things or never took trash and garbage to the dump. This is what our lives are like when we don't call on the Destroyer. Remnants of the past belong in a scrapbook to be revisited and enjoyed, or the scrap heap to be forgotten.

The Destroyer archetype helps us complete the task of establishing our own identity (individuation) by letting go of the *false selves and masks that hide all the parts of our own personalities.* Once we have accomplished that task, we are ready to find out who we really are and claim the ability to achieve intimacy. For that we call on the Lover.

THE LOVEr ARCHETYPE
The part that has passion of all kinds.
GIFTS Passion and ecstasy.
ASK YOURSELF . . . What do I really love and feel deeply about?

"Without love, the Soul does not engage itself with life."

— CAROL S. PEARSON,
Awakening the Heroes Within

———————

"Whether love comes to us as erotic or romantic love, a love for work, for justice, for humanity, or for God, it is a call from our Souls to move away from a disconnected way of living. It requires us to give over our cynicism and believe again. Often in the process, we wake up enough to fear for our Souls at how shallow, loveless, and callous our lives have become. We cannot stay in our old lives, for to do so would be to lose our Souls."

— CAROL S. PEARSON,
Awakening the Heroes Within

———————

If you have ever fallen in love, you know how difficult it is to describe the experience. Other loves and passions are equally difficult to characterize.

Love, like spirituality, is an archetypal force to be experienced, not described or explained. Sometimes, in the grip of the Lover archetype, we need all of the strength of the Ego archetypes to keep us from doing things we might later regret. And, of course we don't always succeed.

Some who have unbalanced egos, like children, often love (or think they love) those who meet only their emotional and physical needs. At other times, the Lover archetype, unbalanced by a strong ego, is easily swept away by sexual passion. A balanced person is capable of finding a *soul mate* and maintaining a special relationship that has to do with shared passions that include and go beyond the passions of the body.

Romantic love, mother love, and agape are each strong and powerful forces that have life cycles of their own. By expressing our loves and our passions we allow the world to see us as we are. We feel the call of the Lover when we fall in love with a person, an idea, a cause, a piece of art or music, or our work.

Through the Lover archetype we become aware of what *moves* us—in a sense, what calls to us on a deeper level. We ask ourselves what is most compelling and important in our lives and realize what we truly value, remembering that values aren't morals, and that it is no better to value making a contribution to world peace than it is to value taking risks. (Morals are the concern of the Ego and the Self archetypes, not the Soul archetypes.) What is important is that we live life in concert with our values and fully aware of our true desires.[6] Initially, we call on the Lover archetype by simply noticing what excites or interests us— what calls forth an emotional charge, or stirs something within us.

Stop for a minute and allow the Lover archetype to sweep through you. Think of a person you love. What is it about them that you love? What are they passionate about, moved by, interested in?

In meeting the Lover archetype, I again make a distinction between therapy and coaching. Often people enter therapy for help with their sexual problems and speak of passion only as it relates to sex. Sexual problems are in the therapist's territory. Depth coaches, however, help clients explore all of their passions. Passions pave the road to purpose; they provide the energy for the vehicle we use on the many journeys through life.

If you have difficulty identifying your passions, use the language of the soul. Instead of asking people about their passions, Carol S. Pearson asks, "What makes your heart sing?" Immediately we are transported to a deeper level. What makes your heart sing? What turns you on? What stirs your soul and brings forth the fire in the belly? For a moment, allow your passions to come to the surface. Are you passionate about ideals and ideas, liberty, justice, rights, fairness? Who are the people in your life about whom you feel passionate? Do you have a passion for art, music, painting, decorative arts or homemaking arts, religion, athletic activities, world affairs, or politics?

Awakening the Lover archetype, discovering what it is we love and feel passionate about, enables us to follow our bliss. Awakening the Lover leads us to our bliss. The important thing is to stay *tuned in* to yourself; observe your daydreams and interests; spend time alone. In *The Power of Myth* Joseph Campbell says, "We are having experiences all the time which may on occasion render some sense of this, a little intuition of where your bliss is. Grab it. No one can tell you what it is going to be. You have to learn to recognize your own depth" (quoted in Leider 1997, 106).

Keep in mind, however, that following your bliss doesn't mean simply going off and doing your own thing. Bliss entails sacrifice, and being in love or being passionately committed to something involves more than pleasure and exhilaration. Ultimately, following your bliss or making a commitment calls for work and discipline— words we seldom associate with the soul—and makes us more aware of the need to strive for balance among the archetypes and the three stages of the journey.

Love and Forgiveness

"Love also comes as compassion, forgiveness, grace. In most religious traditions, this forgiveness comes from God. In a psychological sense, the forgiveness

must come from ourselves. Paradoxically, it is love that calls us to life and deep feeling, and judges our prior lifelessness and lovelessness. It is love that allows us to forgive ourselves so that we can be alive in a new way. And it is compassionate love that allows us to forgive the people we love for not living up to our image of them and for their inevitable inability to fulfill our needs."

— Carol S. Pearson,
Awakening the Heroes Within

—————————

Love is the most powerful force in the world, an infinitely renewable resource that benefits both the giver and the receiver. Stephen Levine tells of forgiving his parents and describes a time when, after years of confrontations and conflict, he faced his father's insults with love and acceptance and experienced a change in his father, and especially in himself, that no amount of arguing or confrontation could have brought about (Levine 1997). Without the Soul archetypes, the Ego, in its attempt to differentiate itself, would have confronted, argued, and tried to make his father understand or appreciate his pain. The Ego without the Soul is unbalanced and doesn't have the strength to transcend personal hurts and losses. The Soul with its deeper connection to all others is able to reach out and love with amazing results.

Coaching the Lover

Forgiving and letting go (combining the Lover and the Destroyer) are two of the most difficult endeavors we face, but at the same time they are the most liberating. They free us from carrying other people's baggage and our own outgrown ideas on our journeys. Although you may choose to forgive someone face to face, the basic forgiveness work takes place inside of you.

Take all the time you need. Think of a person who has harmed you in some way. Create an image of that person and yourself. Become aware of the effects of that harm. You may even want to imagine the harm as a piece of luggage you are carrying. Examine the bag carefully, then slowly and deliberately return it to its rightful owner announcing that you are no longer willing

to carry something that doesn't belong to you.

The act of forgiveness is not the same as forgetting or granting absolution. It is not the same as excusing someone because they were under stress or didn't know any better. Also, we certainly can't forgive someone while they continue to abuse us. Again, forgiveness is not about making excuses. Forgiveness is stating clearly that you are finished with your part, are not taking on someone else's bad behavior, and are ready to move forward carrying your own bags and leaving them to carry theirs.

Think of all of the unnecessary wars and feuds that go on in the world because people are unable to forgive. Undoubtedly, crimes need punishment and people must be accountable for their actions. Horrors such as genocide and holocaust must not be forgotten. But we must also be able to find a way to make reconciliation occur before the world destroys itself.

Perhaps it is too difficult to speak of forgiveness as related to such atrocities as holocaust and genocide. However, in more everyday situations, such as family, school, the workplace, and especially marriage or partner relationships, the inability to forgive causes needless pain and prevents many people from taking their own journeys. The inability to forgive creates bitter angry people who cannot move forward on their own because they are carrying too much baggage.

—————————

A client's journey. A client who engaged in an imagery exercise where she forgave her ex-husband said that she had never before been aware that forgiving was an act that could benefit her. She had always assumed that forgiving would benefit him or "let him off the hook." She was amazed at the feeling of a great weight that lifted from her shoulders when she left the trail she had traveled with him and went off on her own. No longer did she carry the burden of his misbehavior. She continues to use this imagery when she finds herself tempted to reopen old arguments. She has forgiven him, not granted him absolution, because that isn't hers to grant. She has let go.

A client's journey. Sadly, another client refused to forgive his wife for events that took place many years ago. Instead of living life from his essence, he lives from a core of bitterness and resentment. Locked in a hostile dependency he moves toward an old age full of righteousness and martyrdom. He carries her bags, and they are weighing him down. He is not a candidate for coaching. He is alienated from his Soul, and may never even start his own journey.

I like to think of a situation like this as two people each tugging on a rope as in a tug of war. When one person lets go of the rope and walks away, there is nothing the other can do. As long as you hold on to the rope you remain in the other person's power.

Love and Forgiving Ourselves

An essential act that brings forth the Lover archetype is that of loving ourselves. The Caregiver teaches us to take care of ourselves and others, but loving is an activity of the Soul that goes beyond self-care and carries with it the act of forgiving the self and having compassion for oneself (thereby gaining the ability to forgive and have genuine compassion for others). Now that you know that forgiving isn't excusing, forgetting, or absolving, focus on a situation where you need to forgive yourself. Have you neglected someone, been selfish, careless, and rude? It isn't enough for someone else to forgive you, is it? The forgiver has given the burden back to you, and now you must take responsibility for yourself and see to it that you don't do the same thing over and over again. Forgive yourself, accept your responsibility for your own actions, decide what you need to do about it, and do it (make amends if possible). Now allow yourself to experience the sense of peace as the voice of conscience quiets and there is more room in your heart for others. Not to forgive yourself is a selfish act that keeps you ruminating on your own guilt and prevents you from taking the journey.

Many find that forgiving the self helps them to grieve the loss of a loved one. When someone close to us dies, our first thoughts are often about our own behavior toward them: "I didn't tell him I loved him. I wasn't attentive enough. I didn't write, or go to see her in the hospital or call enough or do enough. . . ." Ruminating on these thoughts distracts us from the loss and keeps our attention on ourselves instead of on the one who

has died. At first this may be protective, guarding us from the depth of the loss; but ultimately the loss must be grieved, and we do this by forgiving ourselves and acknowledging our sadness.

Other Ways to Coach the Lover

People aren't always aware of their deepest passions. Different things move each of us. There is no one right thing to be moved by, and very often we are unaware of passions that have been dismissed or denied by others. One way coaches can help clients is by giving feedback or asking clients to notice how they feel when they speak of something they love. We can call clients' attention to a change of expression or rate of speech, and note the light that seems to go on behind their eyes. By paying close attention and being present to the client, coaches can help them awaken the Lover within.

Sherrie's journey. Sherrie spoke of her difficulties with her life and her lack of energy, and for a while it seemed we were going down a well-traveled path of disappointment and physical problems. But when she described a workshop she attended recently she changed before my eyes. I realized how differently I approached her as a coach than I would have as a therapist. At first as she described all of her woes, I automatically began to look for what was wrong with her. I had almost slotted her into a diagnosis and referred her to a therapist, when I was awakened from my trance by the change in her voice and her affect. I remembered that I was guiding her, not treating her. I was trying to help her find her bliss, not heal her wounds.

I began to pay attention to the cues in her speech, her body language, and her affect, instead of the solutions in my head. As soon as I saw these changes, I began to ask questions that deepened her awareness of her interest in a new field. I asked what she was aware of as she spoke and asked: What was it about that talk that excited you? What else? What other things came to your mind after you left the meeting?

She told me of her passion for science and her intense interest in alternative medicine and claimed that this workshop was the first time she had heard these two fields combined instead of contrasted. She began to explore options for following this interest and learning more. She visualized a future where she would use her intellect and her talents to further this cause. Sherrie set the stage for additional Soul work in her working cocoon where she would explore this new enthusiasm and allow it to deepen.[7]

Continuing the journey, we interweave the Seeker, Destroyer, and Lover, our calls, callings, passions, and gifts to help us to discern those things that support the journey and to eliminate those things that don't. For the final strand in the design of the Soul tapestry, we call on the Creator.

THE Creator Archetype

The part that has the ability to open the imagination and bring forth something that never before existed.

GIFTS
Creativity, identity, vocation.

ASK YourseLf . . .
What kind of a life do I long to create for myself personally and professionally?

"Creativity is the ground of any well-lived life. We all create our lives by the choices that are available to us about the ways we live them no matter how circumscribed those choices might be."
— Carol S. Pearson,
Awakening the Heroes Within

"If you do not express your own original ideas, if you do not listen to your own being, you will have betrayed yourself. You will also have betrayed our community in failing to make your contribution to the whole."

— Rollo May,
The Courage to Create

"Creativity remains a powerful source of growth regardless of age . . . creativity which involves affirming life and taking risks demands continuing wrestling with limits amidst changing inner and outer circumstances . . ."
— The Oxford Book of Aging

"I always wanted to be somebody. I guess I should have been more specific."
— Trudy, the bag lady,
In Jane Wagner and Lily Tomlin's play Search for Signs of Intelligent Life in the Universe

The goal of coaching, and of depth coaching in particular, is to help people engage in a conscious and intentional process to create their own lives and live out their own dreams. To become aware of these dreams, we harness the energy of the Creator. The Creator helps us make use of our gifts, take an active role in our evolution as a person, and find our purpose in life. Carol S. Pearson says, "Entering the mysteries of the soul by striving, loving and losing opens us up to grace, to the Muse, to inspiration" (Pearson 1991, 173). Daydreams, fantasies, images, and flashes of inspiration all call forth our creative inner resources. According to Anthony Storr:

> The development of the imagination in human beings has made it possible for them to use the impersonal, as well as the personal, as a principal means of self development, as a primary path toward self-realization. The great original creators are demonstrating one aspect of human potential which can be found in everyone, albeit in embryo form in most of us. (Storr 1988, 75)

Imagination and Composing a Life
The Creator helps us compose a life. Through this powerful process we bring Soul to our lives and experience what it is to feel truly alive. The Creator archetype comes into our professional lives when we create our own professional world, when we find our true selves by discovering what we love and doing what we love to do. To do this requires using the soul's greatest tool—the

imagination. Robert Johnson calls the imagination the "image forming capacity in the mind, the organ that has the power to clothe the beings of the inner world in imagery so that we can see them" (Johnson 1986, 22). The Creator flexes what novelist Vladimir Nabokov called the "muscle of the soul" and brings ideas and images into our consciousness that allow us to create the lives we really want to live.

Using the imagination we can envision what it is that we want for ourselves, set goals, create visions, and design scenarios. In *The Path of Least Resistance*, Robert Fritz states that we can't create until we have a vision of what we want to create. The vision or image precedes the action and sets up a creative tension between where we are and where we want to be, a tension that will not be resolved until we have completed the creation. Within that tension we perform the Soul work that requires enormous exertion of the imagination muscle. Ultimately, the function of the coach is to help clients resolve that tension and close the gap between where they are and where they want to be.

Anthony Storr concurs, "There are good biological reasons for accepting the fact that man is so constituted that he possesses an inner world of the imagination that is different from, though connected to, the world of external reality. It is the discrepancy between the two worlds which motivates creative imagination" (Storr 1988, 69).

Think of the many ways that creative energy flows through us. We paint, draw, sculpt, cook, design, invent, weave, tell stories, and find many other ways to bring something into being that wasn't there before. To a large extent we also have the capacity to imagine a life for ourselves and bring that life into existence as well. Artists and musicians tell us that when they sit down to write a piece of music or create a painting, they have a general idea of what they want the end result to be. The composer says I am going to write an opera based on a story about a bullfighter, or I am going to compose a piano concerto in A Minor. The artist says I am going to create a painting that expresses my horror or contempt at the very idea of war, or paint a seascape that brings to life the turmoil of a storm at sea. The creative process of composing a life is similar—first we envision

what we want to accomplish. We do not want to paint-by-numbers on a canvas prepared by someone else.

Not all of us have the talent to be great creative artists, but all of us have the amazing ability to visualize something that doesn't exist. Often we use this power in a negative way by imagining other people's attitudes about us or by dreaming up the worst possible outcomes for situations. (Think of all of the ways you use your imagination to create worrisome scenarios and invent excuses for yourself.) Using negative self-hypnosis and self-fulfilling prophecies puts us in danger of calling into existence the very thing we most fear.

The good news is that if we can create bad outcomes, we can also create desired ones—as long as it is in our own power to do so and doesn't depend on a random event (like winning the lottery). Sports coaches have known this for a long time, and many a champion athlete spends considerable time visualizing perfect form and concentrating on the desired rather than the dreaded. Race car drivers are admonished to keep their eyes on the road, not the wall, thereby focusing on the finish line rather than potential perils. Tennis players are reminded to focus on the ball and know that when they lose their concentration and think of the worst that can happen at a crucial time (e.g., a double fault), they are quite capable of making it happen. If mental rehearsal of desired outcomes is a successful tactic in sports training, why shouldn't we use it in other aspects of our lives?

**Coaching the Creator:
Problems and Mysteries**

One function of the Creator and our incredible power of visualization and imagination is the ability to change perspective, reframe the issue, or look at events in a different way. Coping researchers have known for years that people respond differently to events when they perceive those events as threats than they do when they see those same events as challenges. It is never too late to bring Soul and the Creator into your life. For example, what is your concept of aging? If, to you, all signs of aging are a threat, you will waste a lot of your time trying to prevent it or pretend it isn't happening. If you see aging as a challenge, you will be actively involved in living your life to the fullest each day. Simply changing perspective or reframing an idea or a situation enables us to get unstuck.

Physical strengths and abilities may wane as we grow older, but our creativity is ageless. Have you ever heard of a writer, an artist, or a composer retiring? Artists live their soul's work, and the soul is ageless. Yet, if we choose, each of us can be an artist in our own lives.

Are you apt to view life as a problem to be solved, or do you see it as a mystery to be embraced? Now is the time to see it as both. Problem solving is an intellectual and rational activity that is concerned with the shared reality of facts and the laws of mathematics and reason.[8] Some things (like building bridges and developing vaccines) are truly problems to be solved, for they rely on the scientific method and linear relationships (although even the solutions to these problems require visualizing and imagination). Dozens of famous problems exist whose answers were found in dreams and visions, e.g., the sewing machine and the double helix. Although we can bring soul to problem solving, bringing problem solving to the soul is more difficult. As Thomas Moore says, "Problem solving is not an effective way to introduce soul into life . . . Soul appears when we shift to a different level of perception altogether" (Moore 1994, 147).

Finding Purpose

The creative process differs in each individual and needs time to incubate. The idea that we can invent ourselves and design a unique life is both exhilarating and intimidating. However, if the structure of a life is to hold up over time, then it must revolve around a purpose. In the Soul Journey or cocoon we have been discovering our gifts (treasures), our passions, and our callings. Now we combine them to find our purpose.

When we live our lives *on purpose* we feel fulfilled. Leider (1997) proposed a way to weave together all of the soulful elements by asking readers to identify their talents (gifts, such as listening, creating, understanding); describe their passions (what do you obsess and daydream about, and what are the areas in which you want to

invest your talents); and identify which environment feels most natural to you (casual setting, one-on-one, alone, in an office, school room, etc.). Your purpose in life is a way to use your gifts to bring forth your passion and to do so in your chosen environment.

If my gifts are teaching, creating, and optimism, I am passionate about helping others to find their direction in life, and my favorite working environments are one-on-one, small groups, or alone, then my purpose might be stated as "to help others find direction in life by teaching, writing, and coaching one-on-one or in small groups."[9] It's up to me to weave together my calls, my callings, my treasures, and my passions to fashion a life that incorporates all of these elements and gives meaning to my Journey.

Betty's journey. For most of her life Betty neglected herself in favor of caring for others—taking the college courses her parents suggested, marrying and deferring to her husband in matters of business, and putting the children's needs first. She hired a coach when her marriage fell apart and she realized that she could not put it back together all by herself. When she took her own journey, she discovered that it was time for her to claim her personal power, identify her purpose, and engage fully in the creative endeavors that made her heart sing.

When Betty called on her Soul archetypes, she found she could now share her creative gifts with the world. She constructed a magnificent lifeline that reached far into the future, with colorful illustrations of specific goals for the next few years. She designed ways to create a space in her home and devised a work routine that would allow her time and the space to follow her dream. As she began to invent her desired life and honor her own gifts and her creativity (she was a fine musician), she found that she no longer had time to put others' needs before her own. Furthermore, she realized that the others in her family were perfectly capable of caring for themselves.

Many coaches have used their creative energies to build coaching practices that combine a coaching practice with their other passions. Some combine coaching with sailing, rock climbing, hiking, or skiing, and follow their own bliss in an environment that inspires both the coach and the client. Can you combine your passions with your purpose?

One of my coaches asked me to identify ten times during my life when I felt *on purpose*— when I felt that I was in the right place, with the right people, doing the right things. Completing this assignment (or field work as some like to call it) was an experience of harvesting the best of the past. I was able to extract the common elements of creativity and gifts of teaching and networking from each of these experiences. I recognized that even though I could never re-create or relive most of those experiences, I could discern from them my purpose and create a new phase of my life.

Once we have a purpose, our whole lives can revolve around purpose like the "wheel impelled from its own hub" (Campbell and Moyers 1988). When you are working *on purpose*, you feel fulfilled and satisfied as if you are doing what you are supposed to be doing. Remember that your purpose is intensely personal, and there is no way of comparing and evaluating purposes. One person may have as a purpose the desire to investigate and find a solution to the problem of world hunger or a cure for AIDS, another to live peacefully in community with others, another to enjoy life and appreciate others, another to create a serene and happy home, or another to bring order to an office or an organization.

In addition, different gods and goddesses call to us at different stages of our lives. Your purpose may change during a lifetime as you move from one developmental phase or life chapter to another—or it might stay the same throughout your life. None of this is cast in stone—life is fluid; only change is permanent.

BALANCING THE DEVELOPMENTAL TASKS OF THE SOUL AND THE SOUL ARCHETYPES

The developmental tasks I associate with the Soul Journey are those of *identity* and *intimacy*. Awakening the Seeker, the Destroyer, the Lover, and the Creator brings to the surface all of the elements of an identity; we know who we are and what we love and find our purpose in the world. This sets the stage for the development of intimacy. Without a clear sense of self, intimacy is impossible because we can't escape the need to continually please others or enlist their approval. Emotional intimacy is difficult to achieve, and most of us have probably connected with very few people in our lives in a truly intimate manner. Even to maintain good friendships is difficult when you haven't found the treasures of your self.

My therapist friend Janet notes that many people confuse intensity with intimacy in that they believe they haven't achieved intimacy unless they deal with intense emotional experiences on a daily basis. These people speak often of "working on the relationship."

I believe that relationships don't have to be hard work, and while couples need to establish ways to compromise, negotiate differences, and share their innermost feelings, analyzing every interaction and emotion may be too exhausting. When each partner has a strong sense of self, intimacy is free and easy, few subjects are taboo, but each one is free to close a conversation without the other feeling hurt. Intimate relationships should not be hard work, and when they begin to feel like work each partner would do well to do some personal inner work—perhaps on the Ego archetypes—before working on the relationship.

Having awakened the archetypes of the Ego and the Soul, we emerge from the cocoon and gain balance once again as we move from the Soul to the Self. Now we take a look at the world around us and determine where and how we can make a difference. The Ego archetypes helped us to look at what we needed to do to take care of ourselves and to fit into the world of others. The Soul archetypes helped us to find our unique selves and initiate the process of individuation. The Self archetypes will show us what we have to do to bring our unique and best selves into the world when we return from the journey. To make a difference we have to do something different, take some action. It is not enough to fit in, to experience, to have insight and experience transformational change. We must also "operate" on the world. To do that, we turn to the archetypes of the Self.

Notes

1. Anthony Stevens (1995) says that, once the theological overtones are removed, the concept of soul is a useful psychological term because it implies the involvement of the transcendent and the eternal and represents all of the psychic equipment operating together.

2. Therefore, we can also look at emotions and symptoms as calls. Hillman (1996) says, "Symptoms in our culture mean something 'bad.' The word itself merely means combination (sym) of accidental happenings; neither good nor bad, that coalesces this with that into an image. As judgment of their value need not be moral, so their province need not be medical. As accidental happenings, symptoms do not belong first to disease but to destiny." He adds, "A symptom wants to be looked at, not only looked into."

3. The Hudson Institute has an effective group method called bouldering in which members of the group give an external voice to each of the voices in one participant's mind. The client has the experience of physically breaking through the boulder and creating and changing the voices to those she needs to support her journey.

4. R. D. Carson (1990) calls the gremlin the narrator in your head who has influenced you and accompanied you all through your life and defines and interprets every experience you have. An essential task of the coach is to help the client escape the influence of the gremlin.

5. Hal and Sidra Stone (1993) have developed an effective method for dealing with these voices in their book *Embracing Your Inner Critic.*

6. Carl Rogers (1961) stressed the importance of congruence between our essence (what we perceive ourselves to be) and our form (as expressed in our behaviors). Rogers originated the concept of "living from the inside out" and thus living one's essence, which has become a central tenet of coaching.

7. Sher and Gottlieb's (1979) book *Wishcraft: How to Get What You Really Want* is a great help to people who need guidance on specific steps they can take to identify and achieve their desires.

8. Dave Ellis (1998) talks about planning by creation and planning by prediction. Predictive planning is based on past events—"the past masqueraded as the future"—and is based on the scientific method and linear relationships. In creation planning you start from nothing and state what you want to have happen in the future.

9. Leider (1997) contends that the purpose of purpose is to organize our lives, provide meaning, follow our hearts, and clarify our calling. He calls purpose the passion that shapes our work life.

CHAPTER 2 WORKBOOK

SOUL ARCHETYPES: FINDING YOUR TRUE SELF

BALANCING THE SOUL ARCHETYPES AND CONTINUING THE JOURNEY

THE REASON WE DON'T TAKE the journey early in life is that we are not yet prepared.

We still examine everything we learn in the light of how others will react to it. We cannot take the journey in a state of dependency. We can be in the world and take the journey at the same time, but we must do deep Soul work separate from our relationships with others.

Start a new section of your travel journal for the Soul archetypes, beginning with the Seeker. In this section, in addition to a section on each of the Soul archetypes with the answers to the exercises below, you might want to include your dream journal, paintings and drawings, and a gratitude journal.

On the Soul Journey, we meditate, write, draw, paint, dream, and give voice to our desires. One writing exercise I like is called *clustering* or flow writing: a non-linear writing process that opens the pathway to the unconscious. The process was devised by Gabrielle Rico and can be found in her book *Pain and Possibility: Writing Your Way Through Personal Crisis* (Rico 1991). This process skirts rational, linear thinking and accesses the unconscious.

THE SEEKER
What do I want? What am I looking for in my life?

_____

_____

_____

_____

_____

Give yourself time to notice your reaction to that question. Stay with any uncertainty and confusion that arises. I have often seen clients burst into tears when asked, "What is it that you want in your life, in your marriage, or in your job?" Clients admit that they really don't know what they want and consider their not knowing as a defect—once again labeling their own responses as wrong. Many people are afraid to want things they cannot have. At least in this exercise allow yourself to name your desires.

Ask the following questions of yourself gently. As you build momentum you can allow your fantasies to soar. Remember times when you felt satisfied, or curious, or content, and allow yourself to be fully present with all of the sensations and images that clothe your desires. Repeat each question until you have exhausted your answers; for example, "I like _____." "Another thing I like is _____." Don't edit or critique your answers. Answer each question with the first word that pops into your head.

I like _____

_____

_____

_____

_____

I feel satisfied when _____

_____

_____

_____

_____

I fully enjoy _____

_____

_____

_____

_____

I want to do more _____

_____

_____

_____

_____

I am happy when I _____

_____

_____

_____

_____

_____

I feel fulfilled when I _____

_____

_____

_____

_____

_____

I feel curious about _____

_____

_____

_____

_____

_____

_____

If I could change anything in my life I would change _____

_____

_____

_____

_____

In my wildest fantasies I have always wanted to _____

_____

_____

_____

_____

Repeat each question at least five times with five different answers.

Calls and Callings

If you already have a calling, ask yourself where and how you became aware of your calling. Wander around inside yourself and listen for the strength and intensity of the calling. Breathe into the calling. Are the voices calling to you now different from the ones who called five years ago?

_____

_____

_____

_____

_____

If you don't have a calling, are there calls you haven't answered yet? Think back to your childhood and recall the passions you had as a child. What were your enthusiasms and interests? Write about yourself in the third person. For example, Susan described herself as a studious child who loved to read and told herself stories each night when she went to bed. However, as she continued to write about "Susan" she remembered more of her grammar school days and re-awakened a love of drawing and painting, color and design. She saw herself as a child making doll clothes and going to painting and drawing classes. The more she wrote, the more she became aware of parts of herself she had lost touch with during the years when she was preoccupied with earning a living and raising a family.

_____

_____

_____

_____

_____

_____

Finding your Gifts, Talents, and Passions

To begin to explore your gifts, talents, and passions, think about or write about the following in your travel journal. Picture the people you envy and admire. Picture what it is that you admire about these people, the work they do, or the pursuits they follow.

_____

_____

_____

Do you have recurring dreams? I often dream of discovering a room in my house that I didn't know was there. I've learned that *to me* this signifies a call to develop or pay attention to a part of myself of which I've been unaware. If that were your dream, what might it signify to you?

_____

_____

_____

_____

Are there songs or song lyrics that you can't get out of your head? At one particularly chaotic time in my life I found myself hearing a song that I couldn't name repeating in my mind. At last I recognized it as the overture to the musical *Carousel*. I realized that something was telling me to "get off the merry-go-round" and find some direction.

_____

_____

_____

_____

Where in your life is there friction and discord? Where you do not walk your talk? Levoy asks what would you preach about if given an hour of prime time TV (Levoy 1997)?

_____

_____

_____

_____

What sort of activities are you drawn to? What do you do well? What are you fascinated by? What are you willing to do over and over again until you get it right? What stories hold your attention? What was your call to your profession? (Was this a genuine call or were you lured into it for other reasons?) If you had it to do over again, what career would you choose? What calls to you now? What part of your job do you look forward to each day? What do you want in your life that is not there now?

_____

_____

_____

What are you looking for in your career and your life? Do you seek security, excitement, or new knowledge and information? Is yours a spiritual quest—a need to find meaning in your life? Take a few minutes to sit quietly and focus on your breathing. Then imagine that you are working in a job that you love or are absorbed in an activity where you completely lose track of time. What do you see yourself doing? What is it about the job or the activity that is satisfying to you? Write a few sentences describing what you found that you liked about the work. When you spend enough time with this exercise you will often find that you don't like certain aspects of your job and do like others. Tease out the elements of the job that are satisfying to you and see if you can apply them to something else.

_____

_____

_____

_____

_____

What is it that you want more of in your life? Sometimes the Seeker comes forth when we list the things we like or when we imagine ourselves as Julie Andrews in *The Sound of Music* listing our favorite things. If you were to sing of your favorite things what would they be? (They don't have to rhyme.)

_____

_____

_____

_____

When you have finished these exercises read them over as if you were reading about another person. How would you describe this person? Write a summary letter to yourself from your Seeker that describes you in the following way:

You are a person who likes _____

_____

You seek an environment that is _____

_____

You have always wanted to _____

_____

You dream about _____

_____

You know that you must take a journey to _____

_____

THE DESTROYER

We call on the Destroyer through ritual, such as acting out the slaying of the dragons and shining light on the shadow. Cutting out the clutter can be a ritual for the symbolic death or destruction of something that can make room for something new to be born. Cheryl Richardson (Richardson 1998) says that we have to cut out the clutter and the energy drainers in our lives to make room for something new (our creations). While this may seem superficial to some, if we look at it symbolically it can be the impetus for big changes in our lives.

Not everyone finds clutter draining, but if you do, find an area of clutter or an energy drainer in your life. What does it symbolize to you? If this task were accomplished or finished what would that mean to you? Un-clutter a small area. Does anything change in your attitude?

_____

_____

_____

_____

Dragons

Now, notice times when you hear the voice of your mother, your father, an overbearing and opinionated boss, a critical teacher, or a sarcastic friend speaking inside your head. Simply notice and breathe. Identify the voices. Who is speaking? What are they saying? Identify your own voice and speak your truth out loud or in writing. When other voices are loud and clear, they drown out the voices of the Soul.

_____

_____

_____

_____

_____

If you are a woman, notice how much attention you pay to magazines that tell women to be painfully thin and eternally young. Have you internalized those images? Do they speak to you when you look in the mirror? What do you have to say in response?

_____

_____

_____

_____

How do you get in your own way? How do you stop yourself from being your best? Describe a time when you sabotaged yourself. Did you ever decide not to sign up for a course because you feared that people would think you were silly for taking a course in flower arranging or auto mechanics, or taking singing lessons or tap dancing at your age? My guess is that it wasn't other people but the internal dragon that placed the boulder in your path. How have you let the dragon drive your bus?

_____

_____

_____

_____

_____

Hold a conversation with your dragon and ask it what it wants of you. Dragon dialogues can be held in self-guided imagery or in writing. Discover what happens when you thank the dragon for the help that it gave in the past and then assign it a new task. Next, see what happens when you choose to ignore it and pay attention to something else. Which method works better for you?

_____

_____

_____

_____

_____

Destroyer and Letting Go

Think of the many ways that you can use the Destroyer to let go of old resentments, of outmoded beliefs, or of the idea that we can know it all or do all things perfectly.

Imagine how it will be when you learn to accept and embrace change as a natural part of life and eliminate the things that don't support your life and your journey?

Name some people, places, things, and attitudes that you need to let go of. Note, I said, "let go of." This doesn't necessarily mean cutting off all contact, but simply letting go emotionally and changing the nature of the contact.

Answer these sentence stems:

I need to let go of _____

_____

_____

If I let go of that I would be _____

_____

One of the ways I might let go would be to _____

_____

_____

I prevent myself from letting go by _____

_____

_____

When we neglect the Destroyer, its shadow forms overpower us. Are there instances where you are overly critical of others who don't share your views? Do you make sarcastic and cutting comments about others to make yourself feel superior? Do you engage in self-destructive behaviors like overeating, drinking, smoking, listening to cruel and useless self talk? Are you able to acknowledge the destructive forces in yourself and your clients? Are you willing to slay the internalized voices of others' authority?

_____

_____

_____

_____

_____

Destroyer and Death

How do you think about your own mortality? If you work as a coach or a guide, how do you help others to think about mortality and acknowledge that all phases of our lives have beginnings and endings? The Destroyer also allows us to cut our losses and leave people and situations that aren't good for us and helps coaches and therapists to say goodbye to our clients when the time comes.[1] The Destroyer helps us eliminate impossible dreams to create the space for the truly possible. What impossible dreams do you need to release? What needs to be cut off or pruned from the garden of your soul so that other things can bloom?

_____

_____

_____

_____

_____

One of the most eye-opening exercises I ever took part in was one in which participants in a workshop were asked to imagine that we had been made aware that we only had six months to live. We were asked to envision ourselves choosing how to spend each day, and to decide how we would now treat all of the people in our lives.

At the time I was in a life transition where, following a divorce, I had gone back to graduate school at age 49. I was living in an unfamiliar city, and four of my five children were scattered all over the country. My financial situation was precarious. I was working at two jobs, going to school, studying, and trying to manage a chaotic household with one teenager at home and the others (and all of their friends) coming back on holidays and summers. At first I thought that, given six months, I would take all of my children and go to some exotic place, or say my tearful goodbyes and go without them on some romantic adventure. Then, slowly, as I visualized myself going through each day, I realized that I loved the life I was leading. I was surrounded by stimulating people, learning new ideas, becoming acquainted with the joys of a good city, and not having to be the daily caregiver for all of the children who were off on their own and growing into themselves. I was able to feel a deep appreciation for what I had and the people who meant a lot to me. Briefly, I was able to tell them the things that I would want to say if I knew that I would be leaving soon. I could easily see the things and people I could eliminate from my life.

Afterwards, I did not become the perfect parent and friend or shower others with unconditional positive regard, but I did hold with me the realization that I was choosing to live my life my way and that I was neither a victim nor a martyr. Try this exercise yourself.

THE LOVER

In some ways these exercises are similar to those for the Seeker and the call, because we are trying to identify ourselves as individuals and, having stripped away the cardboard, now approach our essence.

Ask yourself what "turns you on." Passions are not passive. You don't identify your passion by watching TV or standing in front of the refrigerator asking yourself what you want to eat.

When are you most fulfilled? What part of your life or work makes you feel most alive? What activities absorb you so much that time stands still when you are doing them? What moves you and inspires you and evokes your passions?

_____

_____

_____

_____

_____

_____

What do you love? What brings tears to your eyes? What music moves you? Do you ever talk back to the TV set? What fires you up? What would inspire you to speak publicly in defense of or against an idea or a cause?

_____

_____

_____

_____

Make a list of your passions. Illustrate this with drawings or pictures cut out from magazines.

_____

_____

_____

_____

_____

_____

Forgiveness Exercise

Think of a person you need to forgive. Imagine what it would take for you to do this. Take the time to talk to yourself or to write out a scenario in which you forgive this person in your heart. Do you need to do this in person? What would you gain by that?

_____

_____

_____

_____

_____

Now, think of something you have done that you regret and need to forgive yourself for. Go through the process in your mind and write it out. How will you make amends? What will you do differently in the future? How does it feel to have forgiven yourself?

_____

_____

_____

Next think of someone whose forgiveness you must ask. Create a script for how you want to go about this and decide whether or not you will ask for this forgiveness in person. Remember, we can forgive or ask forgiveness of people who are no longer alive because we have been holding these conversations in our minds whether the person is alive or dead.

_____

_____

_____

Finally, write yourself a love letter from your Lover archetype in which you describe all of your passions, compassions, and deep interests. In the letter, name the ways in which you already express and live these passions. Then suggest ways you will live more from your essence in the future.

_____

_____

_____

_____

_____

_____

_____

_____

_____

_____

_____

_____

_____

_____

THE CREATOR

Write, paint, or draw your future. Write a purpose statement that combines your gifts and your passions. Keep the picture, symbol, or words of this statement on your desk or on your wall. Rehearse your purpose statement out loud and then dare to speak it to another person. Honor the voice of your soul. By determining and naming what you want and saying it out loud or writing it down, you make it more difficult to settle for lesser goals. You begin to participate in life instead of being a spectator or a commentator.

Purpose

We live "on purpose" by continuing to ask ourselves the essential questions: Why do I get up in the morning? Who am I? What am I meant to be doing? After my basic needs are met, what else do I need in my life? Ask yourself each of the following questions:

In what ways do I allow the Creator to express itself in my life?

_____

_____

_____

What is my scenario for my future professional life?

_____

_____

_____

How do I want my life to be in the future?

_____

_____

_____

_____

Where will I be living, who else will be there, and what will I be doing?

_____

_____

_____

_____

In what area of my life have I made creative choices?

_____

_____

_____

What are my gifts? How does my creativity express itself in my life?

_____

_____

_____

_____

Bringing your dreams into your awareness helps you to be open to possibility and less susceptible to self-sabotage. If you want to achieve success and recognition in the field, admit this to yourself at the outset. If you want to be a leader, acknowledge it. If you want to build a private practice, let yourself know what kind of clients you want to work with. If you want to be a speaker, lead workshops, use creative materials (art, music, movement) in your coaching, give form to your creations.

_____

_____

_____

Finally, if you enjoy artwork, create a picture or collage of your soul: illustrate your gifts, passions, calling, and your purpose.

Now, return to your lifeline, fill in some of your goals for the future and describe the legacy you would like to leave.

Notes

1. The way we go about this is a reflection of a balance of the Destroyer with the Ego archetypes. A person with well-developed Ego archetypes will taper off or end a friendship in a respectful way. A person with a less-well-developed ego might be upset with a friend for not meeting her needs and cut that person off abruptly.

Chapter Three

THE RETURN OF THE COACH:
SHARING OUR GIFTS WITH THE WORLD

THE ARCHETYPES OF THE RETURN			
The Ruler	The Sage	The Magician	The Jester

"While spirituality is about bliss, it is also about balance. Without some degree of sacrifice for the greater good, spiritual self discovery leads to plain old self-indulgence."

— ELIZABETH LESSER,
The New American Spirituality

———————

"The issue for us today is not simply to create the unified Self—connecting Ego and Soul, heart and head, male and female—but also to express this Self in the everyday business of our lives."

— CAROL S. PEARSON,
Awakening the Heroes Within

———————

"It is not the separate, transpersonal experience that ultimately matters, but how that experience informs the ways we live our lives. That is what the return is about."

— CAROL S. PEARSON,
Awakening the Heroes Within

———————

THE DEVELOPMENTAL TASKS of the Return are integrity, living by one's values, and generativity, passing on one's learning to other generations. After the Soul Journey, the hero completes the cycle by returning to the community to share his or her treasures. At the end of the Journey, we are clear about our own missions and also have new respect for the missions of others. If we do not return, the Journey has been in vain for, as Hillman says, "We make soul with our behavior, for soul doesn't come already made in heaven, it is only imagined there, an unfulfilled project trying to grow down" (Hillman 1996, 260).[1]

The archetypes of the Self are the ultimate expression of inner balance; through them we express our inner harmony by our actions in the world. The construct of Self includes the Ego and the Soul, the conscious and the unconscious mind, the shadow, and all of the various personas we use to engage the world. The Self is the stage on which the actions of all of the other parts are played—the big picture. It is the part of us that has the ability to unify all the others and to reflect on and think about itself.

Awakening the archetypal energies of the Return—a combination of the Ego and the Soul archetypes working together—allows us to live in a state of integrity, engage the world, and share our gifts. In that way we accomplish the developmental tasks Erik Erikson associated with older adulthood: integrity and generativity. You don't need to be an older adult, however, to live in integrity and share your gifts with others (generativity). We can do this during any period of our lives in which we mark the boundaries of our kingdoms, do our work, continue to learn and pass on what we have learned to others, and, above all, enjoy! In the Return, we take the steps to put our purpose into action and make our visions visible to the rest of the world.

THE RULER ARCHETYPE

The ability to use all of our resources to take responsibility for others as well as ourselves.

GIFTS
Sovereignty, responsibility, competence.

ASK YOURSELF . . .
What is my professional kingdom? What is my personal kingdom?

THE RULER: WHAT IS MY KINGDOM?

"The Ruler as an archetype is about claiming our own power for good and for ill."
— CAROL S. PEARSON,
Awakening the Heroes Within

"As the Warrior needs to learn to fight for what really matters (not just to win) and the Caregiver to sacrifice only for what is essential (not just to be "good") the Ruler needs to learn to use his or her power not just to achieve fame and fortune, but to create a bountiful kingdom for us all."
— CAROL S. PEARSON,
Awakening the Heroes Within

The Ruler combines the archetypes of the Caregiver and the Warrior. When integrated, these aspects of our personalities allow us to escape the bounds of the personal ego and choose how we relate to ourselves. We choose how and with whom we relate in the world at large and in our own occupations, professions, and communities in particular. The Ruler asks: what is my kingdom? what are my responsibilities to my self, my family, my partner, my extended family, my workplace, society, or the world?

Let's begin by looking at personal kingdoms. To call on your personal Ruler, picture people who are or have been the Rulers in the world: the kings, queens, presidents, prime ministers, dictators, warriors, peacemakers, chief executive officers, union leaders, clergy, matriarchs, and patriarchs. These people personify the Ruler archetype. How do you envision yourself in the role of the Ruler? Who best exemplifies your ruling style? Is it Gandhi, Lincoln, Washington, Golda Meir, or Attila the Hun? Is your ruling style the same at home as it is at work? Should it be?

THE RULER IN OUR PERSONAL LIVES

In the Preparation phase of the journey we learned to break the bonds of dependency. On the Soul Journey we achieved the independence that comes with an awareness of a unique identity. On the Return, however, the theme is one of interdependency regulated by the Ruler or the sense of order within each of us. Think of all of the systems in which you orbit—the relationships you have with your self, partner, children, family, work, place of worship, and community. What part of each of these relationships or systems is your personal kingdom? Activating the Ruler can help you determine the nature of these relationships and adjust the balance of your responsibilities to others and to yourself.

Very often we are unaware of our responsibilities and the power we have to choose to make each one of our relationships as interdependent as possible. You can be so enmeshed in each system that you lose perspective and play by other people's rules. One way to get a better awareness of this is to use graphic representations (diagrams, pictures, or objects) that illustrate where you stand with respect to the others in your life and then alter these positions to represent how close or how distant you would like each relationship to be.

Often we need to see and experience (make conscious) our position in each relationship. Virginia Satir used a powerful exercise called family sculpture. In this exercise she asked a person to select others in the group to represent family members and place them in positions that represented their relationship to the client and to each other. Once all the members were positioned—standing, sitting, some close to parents, some far away, etc.—the client could then rearrange the family members into more desirable positions. The exercise enabled a client to experience her own power with respect to others in the family. She realized that she didn't have to stay where someone else had placed her.

Candy's journey. Candy was upset about her relationship with a man who demanded that she make him the center of her life. Even though he lived far away, he phoned her several times each day, expected her to be available for his calls, chose the times they met, and orchestrated all of their time together. She liked spending time with him but resented his interference in her life when they were apart. She wanted to know how to persuade him to change and give her more freedom. Talking to him about the situation and problem solving didn't seem to work. He always had a good reason for his actions.

When I asked her to place a stone on a board to represent herself and to place other stones around her to represent the closeness or distance of each relationship in her life at this moment, she placed his stone right next to hers. When I asked how she would like the relationship to be in six months she placed him at the outer edge of the board—still in her life, but further away than any others.

Until the moment she picked up the stone she had been unaware that she too could play an active role in the relationship. She then devised a plan to change her part in the relationship and carried it out within a month. She decided what she would say and how she would respond to his calls.

She took responsibility for her own happiness and claimed her kingdom. Without realizing it she had allowed her boundaries to be invaded, and she mistakenly believed she had to persuade him to change instead of making the change herself. By picking up and moving the stone she was able to experience her own power in the relationship and, in turn, to appreciate her ability to put all of her other relationships in perspective.

If your relationships are not what you want them to be, you can call on your Ruler. Ask yourself, What is my kingdom with respect to each of the significant relationships in my life? and Where are my personal boundaries? Remember, too, that the boundaries and responsibilities of each personal relationship may change over time. For example, your responsibilities as a parent when your children are toddlers change when your children are teens or young adults. And, although professional boundaries are often determined by legislatures and professional organizations, personal boundaries are (for the most part) determined by the people involved. Because *you* are one of the people involved, you can play the part you choose to play in making the changes.

Remember, you get to play an active part in each relationship, but you only get to play *one* part. In the example above, Candy's friend was acting as the author of the play who wrote her lines and his. Her attempts to make him understand or change his demands went unheard. She woke up and realized that she didn't have to make him understand. She only had to decide what she wanted: to realize what was in her control and then control it—*to rule her own kingdom.*

Coaching the Ruler

Think of the times you try to make others change—to rule their kingdoms—when you really need to be defending or maintaining your own borders. A client asked, "How do I keep my boss from coming into my office and talking to me about personal issues?" The question was restated as, "What can I do to preserve my personal space and keep the proper distance between my boss and me?" She created several ways she could take charge of the situation.

Although there was always the option to appeal to Human Resources if things really got out of hand, she was amazed to find that there were many things she could do to protect her boundaries. She could concentrate on increasing her personal power rather than wasting her energies convincing the boss that he was doing something inappropriate.

Closer to home, you might ask yourself, How close do I want to be to my family? How often would I like to see them? What would I have to do to make that happen?

Clarissa's journey. Shortly after her father's death Clarissa began to feel guilty. Her mother wanted to move in with her, and that didn't fit with Clarissa's plans for her own life. At first she tried to avoid the subject or postpone talking about it, but it stayed in her awareness. The pressure increased as other family members tried to persuade her to go along with mother's wishes by saying that mother was lonely and pointing out that Clarissa was unmarried and had a large apartment.

Clarissa cared about her mother and was concerned that this situation was eroding her relationship with everyone in the family. I asked her if she could envision an ideal relationship in terms of the amount of contact she wanted with her mother. Clarissa created an imaginary videotape of her future and saw herself having dinner with her mother two times each week on days that she, Clarissa, specified. She also saw herself taking her mother shopping, going with her to the doctor's appointments, and checking in with short daily phone calls or emails. Once she could picture that type of a relationship, Clarissa realized that she would be more than willing to take her mother on weekend trips now and then and could fully enjoy the time they spent together.

To get from where she began (a defensive position with the family where no one was satisfied) to where she wanted to go, Clarissa needed to call on her Ruler to outline and follow through on her plans and balance her Caregiver and Warrior. She especially needed to do this when she was in danger of being *guilted* by her mother and other family members for not sacrificing her life to take care of her mother. This required a combination of inner and outer work—inner work to determine what she was honestly willing to do, and outer work to present this arrangement in a positive way to her mother and not back down when and if mother and her siblings weren't happy about it.

Some of the most difficult workplace situations arise where there is no clarity about boundaries and responsibilities: where the organization is nominally organized into teams but there are no team players and everyone plays quarterback; where lines of responsibility and accountability are poorly drawn. Imagine how it would be if you were clear about the boundaries of your relationships. Even in a workplace where you think you have little authority, you always have control over your own behavior.

What would it be like if your responsibilities were clearly defined? What would you be doing differently? What would it be like to redefine each relationship in the best possible light? What archetypal energies do you need to call on?

Anita's journey. Anita works in sales for a large national corporation and is often frustrated by the company policy that creates intense competition within the company sales force. She would like to foster cooperation among her co-workers and believes that cooperation would improve the company's overall market share in a highly competitive industry. However, despite repeated attempts she could not get her message across to the hierarchal management of the company. The situation angered her, and she found herself spending too much time complaining to others and ruminating about how she could convince them that they were wrong.

I asked her to draw a map of the boundaries of her "kingdom" at work and to include within it all of the tasks that were her responsibilities. She also listed her gifts and talents and noted the amount of time she spent doing what she did best (interacting with the customers) versus the time she spent complaining and trying to convince other people that she was right. She found that company policy was outside of her domain, and she could find no way to make herself heard.

Her dilemma now is to see if she can reconcile this situation with her own personal kingdom, her rules for her own behavior, and her use of her own talents. She will have to decide whether to continue working for the company and playing by their rules or find another job more in keeping with her values. The work she will do is deep inner work that she will then bring forth in her actions in the world. She has the power to decide what she will do.

THE RULER AND THE PROFESSIONAL LIFE OF THE COACH: FIVE STEPS IN THE PROCESS

"The Ruler inside of us is always on the lookout for ways to find the potential in the people we influence so that they can use their gifts in a productive way. The Ruler is equally concerned with order."

— Carol S. Pearson,
Awakening the Heroes Within

The Ruler archetype is a constellation of qualities that pertain specifically to our professional responsibilities as coaches or guides. To activate the Ruler archetype and "find the potential in the people we influence so that they can use their gifts in a productive way" is to take responsibility for understanding the principles and practices of coaching and to carry them out in a professional manner.

Figure 3.1 outlines what I call the "Five Responsibilities of the Journey Guide" that I first described in *Finding Your Own True North* (Adson 1999). These are also the tasks and responsibilities of the coach, an outline of the coaching process, and a structure for the coach to rely on as she practices her profession. They constitute a process of coaching that relates to the theory of the hero's journey and will help keep you focused on your professional responsibilities as you work with your clients.

In the sections on the Ego and the Soul you have had an opportunity to complete the first task and have *found yourself* by taking your journey. This step always has to come first, before you ever begin to work with clients. The Ruler archetype is concerned with step five. Step five, following the rules of the road, is actually something to consider throughout the coaching process. (Steps two, three, and four will be considered later.)

The Rules of the Road

Coaches ask themselves: what is coaching? what am I qualified to do? what is my relationship to the client? Having examined one's own worldview, taken a personal journey, and qualified as a coach or other helping professional, we examine the boundaries of our professional kingdoms. How can we be responsible to our clients and to our profession? What are the rules of the road?

What is coaching? I have found no better definition of the role of coach and the concept of depth coaching than in the words of Frederic M. Hudson, founder of the Hudson Institute of Santa Barbara, in the *Handbook of Coaching* (14–20):

Figure 3.1 Five responsibilities of a journey guide

Finding Yourself
Training, philosophical perspective, and personal coaching that allow you to know where you stand so you can help clients find their paths, not yours.

Finding the Client
Assessment and evaluation that help you to experience the world as each client does and find the place on the map where their journey begins.

Deciding on a Destination
Helping the client to set goals and envision destinations.

Choosing the Proper Means of Transportation
Using strategies, assignments, and questions that awaken the internal resources needed to guide each client to a desired destination.

Following the Rules of the Road
Being mindful of the ethics and educational requirements of your profession and your own responsibilities to the client and to society as a whole.

"A coach grounds clients in their core values and beliefs, inspires challenging future scenarios, facilitates optimal choices through visionary plans, and guides the successful enactment of those plans through training, networking and ongoing coaching.

Coaches anchor people to their own internal strengths, and inspire organizations to dream beyond their plans. They apply emotional and intellectual intelligence to the long haul of life and work—a coach grounds clients in their core values and beliefs, challenges them to live and perform at their best. A coach facilitates strategic plans for both the short and the long view.

A coach links inner purpose to outer work . . . with persons groups and organizations. A coach trains mentors and networks. A coach motivates . . . seeks deep results . . . explores new directions . . . invests in the future . . . guides new scenarios . . . forms a link between today's action and tomorrow's results."

The client-coach relationship. The relationship between coach and client is a partnership, an alliance designed to enable clients to move from where they are to where they want to be. A coaching alliance is based on the premise that clients possess inherent inner resources and natural competence, and *dormant capabilities* (the heroes within). This differs from most other professional relationships.[2]

For example, depending on the theoretical background or personality theory espoused by each psychotherapist, the relationship of the therapist to the client can be that of a parent, a physician, a teacher or trainer, or as one human encountering another (*à la* Carl Rogers). Coaching, however, is *always* a client-centered approach in which the needs of the client dictate the roles played by the coach, with two exceptions: the coach is never *in loco parentis,* nor is she a physician/healer. Parenting and healing can occur in the coaching relationship but only happen when coaches enable clients to become their own parents and activate their own healing powers.

Also, there will be times, according to Hargrove (1995), when the coach plays different roles. The coach can play the role of *doctor/ expert,* giving advice when time is short. The coach can be the *guru catalyst* when dealing with executive re-invention and personal transformation. Or in group settings, the coach can be the *learning enzyme* and foster team learning through collaborative conversations and dialogue. Nonetheless, the coach is always in the position of partner and peer, goals are explicit, and the goal of the coach is always to help clients get what they want.

The coach/client relationship, therefore, is far more symmetrical than that of therapist and client, consultant and client, trainer or teacher and client: the coach is a peer—a journey guide— who becomes a powerful ally who helps clients achieve their potential and holds them accountable to their own intentions and goals. Depth coaches regard clients as heroes who are free to choose and are fully capable of change, and they treat them accordingly.

Therefore, even though the content of the coaching relationship is confidential and the coach has the obligation to act only in the best interests of the client—not to take advantage of the client in any way—the concept of a dual relationship is not quite the same as that of therapist and client. Coaches are generally more relaxed about their professional boundaries than are therapists. With the client's permission, coaches meet clients in public places, help with networking, and introduce them to others who can be helpful to them. Executive coaching frequently takes place in the client's workplace, and coaching sessions often occur on the telephone (situations that would be inappropriate in a psychotherapeutic relationship). Nonetheless, the relationship does have boundaries and must come to an end. The contract can make that explicit.

The coaching contract. To ensure that all parties are playing by the same rules, we have to make the rules explicit. The coaching contract is another way in which we evoke the Ruler to make clear the rights and responsibilities of both the coach and the client. The coaching contract states the qualifications of the coach, defines and sets out the particulars of how, when, and where coaching will take place, and states the responsibilities of both coach and client. Contracts can also state what coaching is not. Coaches who are trained or licensed in other fields (lawyers, physicians, psychotherapists, consultants, financial planners) will often specify that this contract is *not* a contract to perform these other services. The contract will state the fees, how they are to be paid, and note the time and place and manner of the meetings. Therefore, from the very beginning of the coaching relationship the client and the coach have a clear understanding of the nature and the boundaries of this relationship.

Within the coaching process itself the coach helps the client call on his or her own Ruler by asking the client to give feedback to the coach about what works and what doesn't. In addition, clients are encouraged to continue to set the agenda by preparing for each session and doing fieldwork between sessions. Some coaches require clients to email a prep sheet to the coach before each session as another way to ensure that the client stays in charge of the agenda.

Other duties of the Ruler. The Ruler coach must also have a clear understanding of the scope of the coaching relationship. An executive coach may focus on coaching as a tool in personal leadership; a performance coach may enable people to achieve specific performance goals. Life coaches and certainly depth coaches consider their clients in the context of their life-span development, relationships, and all the systems in which they are involved. Depth coaches move beyond vocation and career to consider all of life and matters of body, mind, soul, and community as legitimate coaching concerns *as long as that is what the client wants.*

The description given by Laura Whitworth and associates of the Coaches Training Institute describing the four cornerstones of their coactive coaching model is a good example of a Ruler statement:

> The client is naturally creative, resourceful, and whole.
>
> Coactive coaching addresses the client's whole life.

> The agenda comes from the client.
>
> The relationship is a designed alliance.
>
> (Whitworth et al. 1998, 3)

Training and ethics. Finally, to consider coaching as a *profession* and recognize the Ruler's need for order, it is necessary for the coach to be adequately trained (preferably by a qualified coach training institute), and it is *essential* for the coach to conform to a recognized code of ethics such as that of the International Coach Federation.[3] This is not to say that therapists, counselors, and others can't use coaching techniques and approaches. It is to say that whenever we form a professional helping relationship with someone we have an obligation to inform the client of our backgrounds and experience: to state our qualifications and to conform to a code of ethics that protects that client and defines the relationship. We call on the Ruler to define the nature of the relationship at the outset and outline the rights and responsibilities of each party.

MY RULER: FROM THERAPIST TO COACH

Many coaches have difficulty when they make a transition to coaching from another career. Often, lawyers want to give advice, physicians want to heal, teachers want to teach, and psychotherapists want to take care of needy clients. Even though I found I could use many coaching techniques and strategies in psychotherapy, and many psychotherapeutic techniques in coaching, the boundaries of my psychotherapy practice were quite different from those of my coaching practice. When I worked as a psychotherapist, I was in charge of the psychotherapy. I determined the treatment plan or set of outcomes appropriate for the client (although increasingly I resented the intrusion of third-party payers who can determine the nature and duration of the therapy). As a therapist, I frequently worked with clients who were incapable of, or not yet ready, to take their own journeys. My relationship with my clients was not a symmetrical one.

As a coach, at first I had difficulty establishing the boundaries of my coaching kingdom and making the elements of the coaching relationship known to my clients. I am learning to be very clear about the difference in my roles. I continue to begin each coaching relationship with an explanation of what coaching is and how it differs from psychotherapy. It took me a while to realize that I was in charge of this kingdom and could set hours and fees I chose or negotiated. I could establish a business-like working relationship where the client and I collaborated to get the client where he or she wanted to go. It takes constant vigilance for me to keep the agenda in the hands of the client.

THE SAGE ARCHETYPE

The ability to attain wisdom, to seek truth, and to tolerate ambiguity.

GIFTS
Skepticism, wisdom, nonattachment.

ASK YOURSELF . . .
What do I need to learn and how is learning related to wisdom?

THE SAGE: WHAT DO I NEED TO LEARN?

"Sages have little or no need to control the world; they just want to understand it."

— CAROL S. PEARSON,
Awakening the Heroes Within

"The discipline of the sage is to cultivate a desire for truth strong enough to counter the Ego's need to be proven right."

— CAROL S. PEARSON,
Awakening the Heroes Within

"The best thing for being sad . . . is to learn something. That is the only thing that never fails. You may grow old and trembling in your anatomies, you may lie awake at night listening to the disorder of your veins, you may miss your only love, you may see the world about you devastated by evil lunatics, or know your honor trampled in the sewers of baser

minds. There is only one thing for it then—to learn. Learn why the world wags and what wags it. That is the only thing which the mind can never exhaust, never alienate, never be tortured by, never fear or distrust, and never dream of regretting. Learning is the thing for you."

—T. H. WHITE,
Merlin to King Arthur in The Once and Future King

Think of the wisest people you know (or know of): the framers of the constitution, Albert Einstein, Albert Schweitzer, the Dalai Lama, a beloved teacher or mentor. Do you notice that each of these people combines passion and wisdom? I consider the *well-balanced* Sage to be a combination of the Lover and the Seeker: two archetypes of the Soul who are awakened by learning, introspection, and spiritual practices such as meditation, ritual, or prayer. This high-level Sage is contemplative yet also provides the spark for lifelong curiosity and interest and provides the ability to approach work and life with the beginner's mind.

When we awaken the Sage archetype, we develop detachment and the "observing self" so essential to maturity, to meditation, and to the capacity to observe self and other at the same time—an essential component of any helping process, especially therapy and coaching. The Sage seeks wisdom as opposed to vindication. The Sage is eternally curious and is the part of us that helps to keep an open mind. The Sage sees the big picture. Angeles Arrien captured the essence of the Sage in her book *The Fourfold Way* when she claimed that what is necessary for any of us in life is to "Show up, pay attention, tell the truth, and don't be attached to the results" (Arrien 1993).

The Sage is concerned about reality and our ability to look and to listen beyond the pretenses and masks that narrow the scope of our own subjective vision. On the other hand, the Sage understands that there are different kinds of reality. Pearson says, "Every Sage knows the importance of matching methodology to the task at hand. We do not learn about God by quantitative methods. We do not understand demographic patterns through prayer and introspection. Science teaches us about physical realities in the world outside and within us, but is less than useful in exploring the truths of the human heart" (Pearson 1991, 210).

The Sage has to understand the various methodologies and apply them appropriately. The proponents of Appreciative Inquiry make this point when they ask social scientists to judge theoretical accounts not in terms of prediction and control (which serves only to preserve the status quo) but in terms of a theory's ability to generate fresh alternatives and foster dialogue (Cooperrider and Srivastva 2000, 63).

The developmental tasks of the Return are integrity and generativity. On a personal level, we activate the Sage when we examine our values and strive to live our lives accordingly (living with integrity) and when we share our knowledge and experience with others (generativity). The Sage reminds us that learning is a lifelong process and that wisdom is different from knowledge. The Sage seeks to understand the underlying riddles of existence.

To evoke the Sage, learn something about a subject that interests you. Harvest your life for the lessons learned from the mistakes you have made in the past.

The wise coach's journey. A wise coach client described a situation in which she had to handle a difficult group of people in a training program. She achieved her desired outcome, and the clients were satisfied with the results. Nonetheless, she wondered why the experience had been so difficult for her and concluded at first that she didn't want to continue to do this type of work.

As she reflected on the experience and pondered each group member's difficulty, she suddenly became aware that now that the group experience was finished she could learn something from each of the people in the group. She activated her Sage, pictured each person and their salient issue, and asked herself questions. After picturing a woman who held on to traditional values and lines of authority, she asked herself, "How might I be holding on to traditional worldviews and giving up my power to authority figures?" After picturing a man whose problem seemed to be that he

complicated things needlessly, she asked herself, "How might I be complicating my life and making things difficult for myself?" After harvesting her learnings from the experience, she felt a surge of energy.

Values

To live by our values means that we must know what they are, and one way we can make our values clear is by harvesting our life experiences. Whitworth (Whitworth et al. 1998, 121) suggests asking clients questions such as: Where do they [your values] show up? What values do you sell out on first? Which are the most immutable? and Which ones are sometimes neglected?

Identifying values is not something that can be done in one session or with one exercise. We need to identify core values and then use these values as a benchmark for further decisions and actions so that we continue to live life from a core of personal purpose and value. That means *not* making decisions based on pleasing others or keeping the peace.

Finding Yourself Longitudinally on the Journey of Life

"The true measure of your journey through the adult years is not your age. . . . The true measure of your life is where you are in relation to becoming a complete person."

— F. M. Hudson and P. D. McLean,
LifeLaunch: A Passionate Guide to the Rest of Your Life

THE SAGE ARCHETYPE
ASK YOURSELF . . . **Am I at the morning, afternoon, or evening of my life? What factors and developmental challenges does each age bring?**

As we coach individuals and take our own journeys, it helps to keep in mind the ages and stages of life. Each age brings with it a special set of tasks and challenges. As you prepared for and participated in the Soul Journey, you learned a lot about your inner life and the timeless aspects of the Soul archetypes. Now, you can put yourself in perspective on the chronological journey through life. In recent years, the pace of life has increased so rapidly that each generation has to reexamine its views of maturity and aging. We begin by asking ourselves where we are on our personal journey through the years.

Throughout the workbook exercises in this book I have asked readers to locate themselves on a chronological lifeline, noting where they have been and also where they have yet to travel on this journey of life. Look at your lifeline and think of it in terms of the seasons. Are you in the spring, summer, autumn, or winter of your life?[4] More importantly, where are you *in relation to becoming a complete person?* Be aware that each age can bring something new and potentially exciting if you open yourself to flexibility and possibility.

In *The Power of Purpose: Creating Meaning in Your Work and Life*, Richard Leider envisions life as a form similar to that of the chambered nautilus who continues to grow and outgrow his chambers. At each developmental stage, new questions arise to answer:

Childhood = what do I want to be when I grow up?

Adolescence = where do I fit?

Young adulthood = what is my calling?

Middelescence = who have I become as a person?

Young older adulthood = How do I measure my success as a person?

Elderhood = what value—legacy—have I added to people's lives?

(Leider 1997, 53)[4]

So far, as we awakened the archetypes of the Ego and the Soul we pondered the questions associated with childhood, adolescence, and young adulthood. In general, the morning of our adult lives is the time when we prepare for the journey by leaving home and getting an education or training for a profession, live out (or rebel against) the expectations of others, seek a mate, and begin a family of our own. Today, however, putting chronological ages on these stages is difficult when so many young people remain dependent on their families well into their twenties, or delay starting a family to pursue a career, while others leave home or bear children at too early an age and often postpone the Journey indefinitely.

Nonetheless, the afternoon of life is the time when we take the Soul Journey and begin the initiation into our true individuation. This is the time the hero finds an identity and lets go of the dependency of youth. Chronologically, this can take place any time from early adulthood to middle age and even into early older age. It is hardly ever too late. Most of us take more than one journey to the Soul. However, whatever your age, when you return from the journey it is time to consider the special responsibilities and questions of adulthood and elderhood.

Schachter-Shalomi describes elderhood as a time of "reflecting on our achievements, feeling pride in our contribution to family and society, and ultimately finding our place in the cosmos" (Schachter-Shalomi and Miller 1995, 23). All of these are matters of deep concern for the Sage. No matter what age you are, now is a good time to look at your life-span as a whole, think about how long you would like to live, and begin to plan for old age and the legacy you want to leave after you are gone.

COACHING ELDERS

"Jung noted that after midlife, when the rising sun has established its position at the zenith and begun its descent toward evening, people should begin spending more time contacting their inner selves. We begin individuating, becoming and expressing the unique selves that we are. This curriculum of life's second half involves more than the completion of our biological imperative. It involves the evocation of soul and spirit."

— Rabbi Schachter-Shalomi,
From Age-ing to Sage-ing

"... a human being would certainly not grow to be 70 or 80 years old if this longevity had no meaning for the species. The afternoon of human life must also have a significance of its own and cannot be merely a pitiful appendage of life's morning."
— CARL JUNG,
The Stages of Life

"The Oxford Book of Aging is guided by the understanding that later life in the West today is a season in search of its purposes. . . . Thus our era offers new opportunities for reclaiming the moral and spiritual dimensions of later life, for bridging the gap between existential mystery and scientific mastery, for reconciling the modern value of individual development with the ancient virtues of accepting natural limits and social responsibilities."
— OXFORD BOOK OF AGING

The Developmental Tasks of Adulthood

We return from the journey many times during a lifespan and, as I have said earlier, I don't believe that Erikson's psychosocial developmental tasks necessarily coincide with the ages he assigned to them. However, our coaching clients are adults, and an important and often neglected phase of adult life is that of elderhood. Now that people's active and productive lifetimes are lasting longer and longer, we need direction and encouragement to enter into this phase with the energy and enthusiasm it deserves. We call on the Ruler and the Sage to help us share the gifts of our wisdom and experience and to teach and mentor those who will share our legacy.

I identify the developmental tasks of the Return as Erikson's stages of generativity vs. stagnation and integrity vs. despair. The task of generativity is one of transcending one's own needs to sharing one's gifts. Generativity is a form of altruism—going beyond the benefits to one's own children and caring for the next generation and the future, by teaching and mentoring, for example. The task of integrity is the attainment of wisdom: the wisdom of practical skills, the wisdom of psychological insights, the wisdom

to outwit the dragon rather than slay it. To acquire integrity we live by our values; we self-confront and reflect. We own all the parts of ourselves, and ultimately we face the shadow. For those who have not yet reached the chronological ages of elderhood, these are experiences to anticipate, not tasks to dread.

Similar developmental tasks are found in many spiritual traditions as well as in the writings of modern-day stage theorists. These tasks are also described in myth and fairy tale in all cultures. In a study of elder fairy tales from diverse cultures, Chinen (Chinen 1989) found the tasks of later life to be: self-reformation and self-transcendence, wisdom (practical rationality), integrity, the return of wonder, and spiritual enlightenment.

A New Perspective on Aging

Recently, the late afternoon and the longer and longer evening of life are beginning to get the attention they deserve in our culture—a culture that has long been oriented towards eternal youth. In the last fifty years, advances in medicine, nutrition, and science (hormone replacement, gene therapy, organ replacement, stem cell research) have added years to our potential life spans. What is even more important is that the fortunate among us (those with enough money and good health) do not think of themselves as old; they are active, involved, and not marginalized.

Because people are living longer, the epicenter of economic and political power is shifting. Coaches can help clients decide how to spend these extra years. How we *choose* to become elders may become the most important challenge we face in our lives.

In *America the Wise*, Theodore Roszak asks us to think of the extra years of life as a resource. He notes that

> "Never before have people over 60 had so much wealth or exerted so much political influence. . . . They are avidly pursued for university coursework and museum shows, they are the most reliable season ticket holders for the opera and the symphony. . . . For the first time in modern history, the senior population is

beginning to be treated as if its tastes and interests matter." (Roszak 1998, 10)

Roszak also notes that never before have so many physically and mentally healthy and fitness-conscious people had access to so much health care. He urges those who possess technical skills, professional training, and intellectual astuteness to consider staying on the job beyond legal retirement age.

From "Age-ing to Sage-ing"

"An elder is a person who is still growing, still a learner, still with potential and whose life continues to have within it promise for, and connection to, the future. An elder is still in pursuit of happiness, joy and pleasure, and her or his birthright to these remains intact. Moreover, an elder is a person who deserves respect and honor and whose work it is to synthesize wisdom from long life experience and formulate this into a legacy for future generations."

— BARRY BARKEN,
founder of the Live Oak Living Center

In a remarkable book called *From Age-ing to Sage-ing* (Schachter-Shalomi and Miller 1995), Rabbi Schachter-Shalomi proposes a "new model of late-life development called *sage-ing*, a process that enables older people to become spiritually radiant, physically vital, and socially responsible 'elders of the tribe.'" He says we can move from age-ing to sage-ing through life completion; that is, by recognizing that we are going to die and completing our lives. He urges elders to live their lives completely and become what they were meant to become. He calls on them to live consciously and thereby free up the energies needed to defend against death by encountering their own mortality. These are important considerations at any age but especially in troubled and uncertain times. I see this as yet another call to the Journey.

To do this Schachter-Shalomi suggests that we use the tools of the *consciousness* movement, Buddhism and other mystical teachings, humanistic psychology, transpersonal psychology, and mind-body medicine—methods and techniques

congruent with the concept of depth coaching. Schachter-Shalomi asks elders to do their philosophic homework by asking the questions: Why am I here? What is my place in the universe? What is my purpose? What are my beliefs?

No matter how old you are, these are significant questions. Ask yourself: Why am I here? What is my place in the universe? What are my beliefs? What is my purpose? Is it time to take a new Journey?

Having reached a state of self-transcendence and self-confrontation or emancipated innocence does not mean that the elder should only sit and contemplate, but rather that he or she can be in the world in a different way. Most who write about aging and creative aging suggest that elders become role models of human development; that they stay in the workplace by adopting a service orientation; that they mentor, advise, teach, and take part in all manner of community service organizations—that they return *again and again* from the Journey.

THE PROFESSIONAL SAGE ARCHETYPE: LIFELONG LEARNING

"In a time of drastic change it is the learners who inherit the future. The learned usually find themselves beautifully equipped to live in a world that no longer exists."

— ERIC HOFFER

THE SAGE ARCHETYPE
ASK YOURSELF . . . **Am I learned or a learner?**

"Adults who are truly alive are always learning. Learning for them is an attitude, a habit, and a way of life. To learn is to turn problems into investigations, and crises into opportunities."

— FREDERIC M. HUDSON
AND PAMELA D. MCLEAN

Look around at the changes in the way we learn and think about learning that have occurred in just the past few years. The technological changes are amazing and evident, but other changes are equally impressive. We live in a world of such dazzling change that Peter Vaill describes it as "permanent whitewater." He notes that to survive we must continue to have learning experiences that are self-directed experiences in which we learn by doing, feeling, and making mid-course corrections as we go along (Vaill 1996). No longer is it enough to sit passively in classrooms, listen to lectures, and study from books and notes. Now you can try things out, take new roles or viewpoints, create learning opportunities for yourself, and take classes on the telephone and the Internet.

Coach training programs are good examples of putting new ways of learning into practice; trainees don't learn about coaching, they learn by being coached, by coaching, by putting into practice what they have learned in their extensive readings, by participating in intensive, in-person group experiences, and in follow-up groups and individual teleconferences. Much of the learning is self-directed and results are evaluated by presentations, portfolios, and performance rather than by examinations and term papers. As Frederic Hudson says, "Learning isn't just for kids."

The Learning Questions

In their classic book *LifeLaunch* (Hudson and McLean 1996) and in LifeLaunch™ workshops and coach training programs at the Hudson Institute of Santa Barbara, Frederic Hudson and Pamela McLean emphasize the importance of the concept of life-long learning. They ask the individual (the learning organism) and the organization (the learning organization) to consider seven questions that conceptualize the learning process as discovery, awakening, experience, and reflection. These are tools needed to master the developmental tasks of the adult, as opposed to the tools that emphasize only the acquisition of skills, knowledge, and information we once needed to prepare for the Journey. These questions are:

1) If I am going to master the future I really want, what do I have to unlearn; what patterns do I need to break?

2) To be at my best at this stage of life, what new information and knowledge do I really need, and what don't I need?

3) To be alive and purposive in all that I do, what life skills do I want and need to develop?

4) To improve at this time in my life, what technical skills do I need?

5) To keep my life aligned to my values and leadership roles, what do I need to learn?

6) At this time in my life, where are the learning environments and resources that I need?

7) At this time in my life, who are my teachers and mentors? (Hudson and McLean 1996, 110–115)

These questions can be asked of each coaching client but first must also be asked of each coach; and the answering of the question evokes the Sage. Take some time to answer these questions with respect first to your personal life and then to your profession.

Learning styles. A final consideration is *learning style*. There are many different ways to learn, and we can't assume that everyone learns the same way we do. Examine your own learning style. Are you adept at learning from books, lectures, tapes, or experiential learning? Are you highly visual? Do charts and graphs help you or turn you off? Learning is not a passive activity and certainly not synonymous with memorizing. You have to act on what you have learned, and that action is a function of the Return. Pay attention to your clients' individual learning styles as you work with them and certainly pay attention to your own. Most people need to have a change of experience before they completely assimilate new information.

The philosophy of the Sage. Frederic Hudson summarizes the basic tenets of his coaching philosophy and the wisdom of the Sage when he writes:

"Life recurs in circular, self-renewing processes, measured by cycles and chapters, not linear accomplishments.

Life is best lived from the inside out. To stay on course you need to be value driven and purposive.

Learning isn't just for kids. The way to stay awake through the adult years is to continue to gather new information, enhance the human skills of speaking, writing, listening, and persuading, caring and managing conflict, acquire new technical skills, and learn more about your values and become a leader.

Change is endless and the journey is more important than the destination." (Hudson and McLean 1996, 34–38)

MY SAGE: WHAT DO I NEED TO UNLEARN AND WHAT INFORMATION DO I NEED?

Of all the questions above, I found this question most difficult to put into action. Even though I had worked long and hard on the journey guide concept, making the transition from therapist to coach forced me to examine even more closely the way I work with my clients. I found that I often had an agenda for my coaching clients. I caught myself analyzing and interpreting their words and actions. I continued to fall back on old habits and wonder why clients were behaving the way they were. That practice prevented me from focusing on the way in which clients could achieve their goals. I had to be conscious about actively letting go of old theories and judgments and retrain myself to listen with my whole being and with an open mind. I also had to let go of my tendency to take care of my clients and had to remind myself continually that my clients were adults who could well take care of themselves.

I did this by working with a mentor coach and enrolling in additional coach training that guided me into a self-directed learning mode, that in turn made me think about why I wanted to learn what I learned and how I could put it into practice. This experience made me see the superficiality of many of my previous modes of learning. I became aware of (and embarrassed by) how often I wanted to impress others with what I knew and times when I wanted to have the right answer rather than simply being open to new knowledge and trusting myself to do the right thing. I remind myself daily to focus on curiosity rather than certainty. I do not have the right answers to other people's questions about themselves. As John Whitmore says, "It is hard,

but by no means impossible, for an expert to become a good coach" (Whitmore 1996, 38). I'm letting go of being the expert.

THE MAGICIAN ARCHETYPE

The ability to transform what needs to be changed by acting on our own visions.

GIFTS
Personal power.

ASK YOURSELF . . .
What do I need to change and how can I help others to change?

THE MAGICIAN: WHAT DO I NEED TO CHANGE?

"The power of the Magician is to transform reality by changing consciousness . . . without the Magician . . . the kingdom cannot be transformed."

— CAROL S. PEARSON

". . . my commitment and their commitment became an alchemical chamber in which transformation would occur, often in magical and mysterious ways."

— ROBERT HARGROVE

The Magician is a combination of two powerful archetypes: the Creator and the Destroyer. When we call on this archetype we bring into being things that never before existed and let go of those things that no longer add value to our lives and the lives of others.

In our personal lives the Magician enables us to face our fears instead of denying them. We call on the Magician when we marvel at those who have dared to make their dreams come true: Lindberg who first flew across the Atlantic, Walt Disney whose magic has transformed our consciousness, and Milton Erickson, M.D., whose skills and powers of observation enabled him to change the practice of clinical hypnosis.

The Magician embraces change, transformation, and transition. Even though we might give lip service to the notion that life is a series of changes, most of us have difficulty coping with the rapidly increasing pace of change. We often need help to make the transition from one stage or chapter of life to another. A coach provides that help.

THE MAGICIAN IN OUR PERSONAL LIVES

"You can't roller skate in a buffalo herd, but you can be happy if you've a mind to."

— ROGER MILLER,
"You Can't Roller Skate in a Buffalo Herd"

In our personal lives we survey our kingdoms and ask, What do I need to change? Think back over your life and recall how you looked forward to change when you were a child. How has your attitude about change evolved over the years?

Ask yourself. What do you need to change about your self or your relationships with others that will add value to your life and to the world (or at the very least will make life less stressful)? What archetypes need balance? What are your beliefs about change? What do you need more of or less of? Look back over the sections in the book about the Ego and the Soul and see if you have changed as you have taken this journey.

Do you understand how much power you have to make changes in your life? We can't change facts, but we can always change perspectives. We can break patterns and old habits and stop beating our heads against the wall (trying to change the wall but succeeding only in damaging our heads).

THE PROFESSIONAL MAGICIAN: THE COACH

The journey of the coach, therapist, counselor, or journey guide is the journey of the Magician. Changing consciousness and awareness—awakening—is what we do. We change others by first becoming true to ourselves. We calm others by being calm ourselves and motivate others by being motivated. As coaches we also have an obligation to become familiar with the many change strategies that connect people to their own paths and to their own powers (their archetypal forces).

The very power to name can be magic and, when used with care, can be a transforming force. When used carelessly, however, this power can be damaging. Look at how much harm some psychologists did when they named many ordinary feelings and situations as diseases and turned health into illness. Name-calling is a powerful thing. The coach can help people reframe, rename, and see things with a different perspective with amazing (seemingly) magical results. The coach does this not by working magic on clients, but by teaching clients to be magicians in their own lives. Coaching is not something you do *to* people but something you do *with* people.

The unique nature of the coaching relationship calls for knowledge of the fundamentals of change, a profound respect for the client, and a sincere belief in the client's ability to change. If you don't believe with all of your heart that a client is capable of change, don't agree to work with that client.

The Magician is also trying to reveal in the ordinary world the truth of the non-ordinary dimension. A simple example of this is helping clients discover their purpose or calling. At a deeper level this may be manifesting heaven on earth—ideal forms expressed in the material world—by finding the real nobility of the clients (deeper values and special gifts) and helping them to express these in the way they live their lives.

The coach—as generalist and change agent—must also have some personal characteristics not always required in other professions. These include intense curiosity, the ability to inspire, creativity, imagination, intuition, and a passion to help others grow and learn—to help others find their own paths. Some of these characteristics can be learned, but others cannot. If you don't have passion, you can't fake it. Find another profession. This is not your calling.

However, none of these warm and fuzzy attributes of the coach are important if coaching doesn't result in the client achieving his or her goals. This is what the Return is all about, and this is what coaching is about. I can develop my Soul and my identity and find my purpose in life, but I must then come down from the mountain-top (or return to the kingdom) and carry out my purpose. Our goal as depth coaches is to help others find themselves, take their journey, and get the results they want; and for that we must be skilled in the use of the tools of the trade.

The Magician's Magic Wands

As I stated earlier, the concepts and techniques used in coaching are related to many of the newer, outcome-oriented action- and competency-based therapies that emphasize shifting contexts, systems thinking, solution orientation, and externalizing the problem.

In addition, coaches also use techniques and tools from the management and organizational development literature that emphasize systems thinking, taking the long view, holding all the points of view in mind at the same time, learning by experience, exploring current reality, developing a view of the future versus solving the problems of today, and self-managed learning (Weisbord and Janoff 2000).

To keep all of these ideas in a proper framework and know when to use each tool, I turn to my framework of the duties and responsibilities of the journey guide listed in the section on the Ruler.

MORE TASKS OF THE COACH

You have found yourself, taken a personal journey to achieve archetypal harmony, balance, and fulfillment, and examined the rules of the road. Now you can give your full attention to the tasks of finding the client, helping the client decide on a destination, and providing a proper vehicle to help the client get where she or he wants to go.

Finding the Client

Before you can get where you want to go, you first have to know where you are.

> Client to travel agent: Tell me how I can get to Chicago by Saturday?
>
> Travel Agent: Where are you now?
>
> Client: I don't know.
>
> Travel Agent: Then I'm sorry but I can't help you.

Many clients have a good idea of where they want to go and where they have been but are really not too sure where they are. If you have ever been lost in a shopping mall, you know that the diagram showing the layout of the mall would be useless without the "x" that marks the spot to show you where you are. In the same way, when you take a hero's journey you need a map that shows not only where you want to go but also where you begin.

Most often clients come to coaches with a general idea of what they want: a better job, a happier relationship, a more productive workforce, a sense of meaning, or an increased zest for life. Our task is to help them make this goal, dream, or vision more explicit and coach them on the actions they might take to get where they want to go. We coach the gap between where clients are and where they want to be. To do that we have to know both parameters.

People usually enter a coaching arrangement with some specific goals, but often follow up with some roadblocks, such as, "I have to make a decision about taking a new job, and I have always had trouble making decisions" or "I would like to find a life partner and get married again, but I was so burned the first time that I don't think I'll ever trust another woman." If we view each situation as a problem to be solved and then look backward to seek the cause, we will probably not move forward very quickly. Certainly life presents problems: broken bones need to be set, bills need to be paid, mental and physical illnesses need to be medicated; but then what? From the outset we want to frame coaching goals in a nonproblematic way.

Solution-focused therapists have long taken more traditional therapists to task for locating the problem within the individual, saying, "the person isn't the problem, the problem is the problem." As coaches we want to locate the problem outside of the client but locate the *solution* within the client.

Many clients will be vague about describing their present circumstances (the present scenario) and have equally vague ideas about the future. They will begin with a few complaints such as, "I am stuck, I am going around in circles, I am blocked in my writing, I hate my job, I feel empty."

How to find the client. As we listen and

acknowledge, we make note of the assets the client has to work with and collaborate with the client to develop a factual description of his or her present situation or scenario. Even our initial comments and questions can contain the seeds of Appreciative Inquiry or a solution-focused approach.

In the process of coaching the intervention begins with the first questions asked, and the inquiry is an intervention. Coaching questions are seldom asked for the purpose of informing the coach; they are asked for the purpose of awakening the client.

Once the coaching contract has been established, there are many ways to find the client—so many ways, in fact, that every coach can find or devise an assessment model that fits her style and philosophy. Keep in mind, however, that we are looking for assets and strengths (treasures) of the individual—possibilities rather than liabilities. And we seek ways to enable each individual client to appreciate, acknowledge, and use these assets. Therefore, unlike personality profiles and standardized psychological assessment instruments (assessment tools that compare people to others on personality traits, symptoms, intelligence, or ability), coaching assessments focus on the individual's strengths or preferred way of interacting with the world and with others. Depth Coaches use instruments like the *Myers-Briggs Type Indicator®* (*MBTI®*) instrument or the *Pearson-Marr Archetype Indicator™* (*PMAI™*) instrument. The *PMAI* is an instrument designed especially for use with the archetypes of the hero's journey. It provides a graphic representation of the client's archetypal balance at the present time. These instruments provide information that is useful to the client and the coach and do not stereotype, diagnose, or label the client.

Coaches can use any assessment method or instrument that will help the client become more aware of his or her situation, capabilities, and possibilities. We might ask, Who is this person? What are the client's dreams and aspirations? How does the client look at life? What does the client want out of this relationship? or How can we best help the client? We help the client to find himself and ask for continuous feedback about what works and what doesn't.

To have a good sense of the client and identify the client's present position on the journey before he or she begins the journey, most coaches ask clients to complete a packet of self-report questions before the first session. Answering these questions begins the coaching process and helps clients clarify their current situation and their goals.

In the process of finding the client the coach will use her skills of listening, empathy, and acknowledgment and set the stage for a trusting relationship. These skills are well described in Egan's classic, *The Skilled Helper* (1998), in Havens' *Making Contact: Uses of Language in Psychotherapy* (1988), in *Finding Your Own True North* (Adson 1999), and in the literature on solution-focused and possibility therapies, especially *A Guide to Possibility Land* (O'Hanlon and Beadle 1999). Additional processes and procedures of coaching, along with an excellent reference list, are found in the comprehensive *Handbook of Coaching* (Hudson 1999).

Generally, coaches do not require a detailed and lengthy history of the client, although at some point the coach may use a form of life review as a tool to help the client put his or her life in perspective, harvest strengths and successes, and reconnect with youthful enthusiasms or passions. The type of lifeline described in this book, on which clients note the important events of their lives and identify where they are now, make plans for the next stages of their life, and state the way they want to be remembered, is a simple way to help clients organize their experience over time and create a visual reminder of the ups and downs of life over the lifespan.

In addition, clients also need to have a sense or an image of their place in each of the systems in which they are involved. They will see a way to see themselves in relationship to the self, the family, extended family, friends, workplace, and community—a map of the context of their lives. We can do this with diagrams, or with objects that we manipulate to represent ourselves and others. Examples are the stones on a board referred to previously, or chairs or other pieces of furniture arranged around the room to represent closeness and distance between the client and the others in each system in their lives. Although at any given time we may be working with only one person, that person's life is a part of many systems, and each person plays a different role in every system of which they are a part. Visual props like the lifeline and experiential exercises are essential tools that take clients to a nonverbal level where they participate actively in the coaching experience. These props provide both client and coach with the "x" that marks the spot where the client begins the journey.

Deciding on a Destination

One of the important tasks of a coach as a guide on the journey is to help clients decide on a destination. Coaches generally ask how people want things to be rather than what they want to accomplish. For this task we call on the Creator aspect of the Magician.

Because the coaching inquiry views most situations as mysteries rather than problems to be solved, we begin with a question such as, What is it that you really want to see happen in your life, your organization, or your relationship? Following the tenets of Appreciative Inquiry and brief solution-focused therapy, coaches "plant the seeds of change in the first question because they believe that human systems grow in the direction of their deepest and most frequent inquiries" (Cooperrider, Sorenson et al. 2000, 7). However, inquiries like these take time to answer; they require reflection, meditation, journaling, and visioning.[5]

The Magician asks the *miracle question* and uses the results of that question to create goals that arise from the center of the client's being. The miracle question is, If you awoke tomorrow to find that while you slept a miracle had occurred and you were living the life of your dreams, what would that look like (de Shazer 1990)? Bill O'Hanlon uses a technique he calls *videotalk* and asks, If we had a video of your life when it is what you want it to be, what would it look like? What would you be doing? What kinds of people would be around you? What would your environment look like? (O'Hanlon 1996).

The Magician calls on the Creator archetype by using one of coaching's most effective tools: *visioning*. We help clients create a picture (for themselves, their relationships, or their organizations)—a detailed image of what they want to have in the future. Using all of our creative powers and the tools of the imagination, we ask clients to make comprehensive images of desired goals. We ask them to picture what it would be like to live the life of their dreams. Then we ask them to project themselves into the picture, see the sights, hear the sounds, smell the smells, feel the feelings, and name the activities they're doing and the other people who are involved. From here, clients can go on to plan the steps they need to take to make that dream into a reality.

The coach might ask, for example, What are you willing to risk to make this vision a reality? What are you willing to give up? How do you keep yourself from reaching this goal (e.g., finishing your dissertation)? What would it be like to have finished? Specifically, in what way will your life be different then? What are the dragons and boulders that block your way? Other questions require the making of mental pictures and a connection with feelings. What will it be like when you reach your desired outcome? What about this makes it so terrifying to you? Where do we go from here? How will you know when you have reached your goal? (These are the questions from solution-oriented therapy, possibility therapy, and Appreciative Inquiry.)

Charles's journey. Charles agonized over a decision about whether or not to retire. He had exhausted his problem-solving approach with pros and cons and risks and benefits, but he still couldn't decide. I asked him to call on his Creator to envision and compose for himself a picture of the life he would like to be living in five years. As he abandoned his dilemma and dreamed, wrote, and meditated, his focus changed. He saw himself living a more active life in which he continued to learn, teach, and help other people. He envisioned a life with time for his family and stimulating friends. He saw himself going back to school. He reconnected with his passions and pictured them as an integral part of his life.

He is now taking actual steps to face an exciting challenge ahead that will enable him to bring his real self to the world instead of retaining the identity bestowed on him by his job. He knows that there are sacrifices involved, but he is excited about the future. His focus has shifted from the decision about whether or not to retire to the search for a way to live the life of his dreams. He may or may not choose to retire from his current job right now, but he will not retire from his life. Charles was asking himself the wrong question.

Providing the Proper Vehicle to Help Clients Get Where They Want to Go

The most important tool of the coach is the *powerful question*. It is the question that evokes the archetype, changes the inner experience, and leads the client to take the action that gets him where he wants to go. The nature of the coach's question will determine the level on which coaching takes place. In depth coaching the most useful is the powerful question that directs clients' attention inward and forces introspective answers or observations that transform clients' experience of themselves. Whitworth describes this as "inviting clients to look—not just with their brains, but with their heart, soul, and intuition, into places that are familiar but seen with new eyes, and places they might not have looked before" (Whitworth et al. 1998, 69). I call it *awakening inner resources or archetypes.*

When a client expresses fear of a probable outcome, master Magician therapist Bill O'Hanlon will often ask, "So What?"—a question that may sound flippant but not when asked with respect, a question that forces the client to look at the matter in a different way. Another familiar therapy question is "What is the worst thing that can happen if you do that (or don't do that)?" This question helps a client imagine a worst-case scenario, which often isn't all that bad. Questions like these direct a client to his or her interior process or narrowly focus outward attention. Answering the question becomes an experience rather than an intellectual exercise.

My emphasis on depth in the coaching relationship doesn't mean that I see other types of coaching conversations as unimportant. As Frederic Hudson says, coaching is about both *doing* and *being* (what I would call *performance and existence coaching*). Once we figure out who we are, we need to do something different. We need to perform in some way that brings our essence into the world and accomplishes what we desire.

Therefore, even in depth coaching the coaching conversation can take place on many levels. Hargrove defines these levels as single-, double-, and triple-loop learning (Hargrove 1995). The single loop represents incremental learning, the double loop a reframing that includes both actions and strategy, and the triple loop shifts the context of learning and creates fundamental change. Flaherty (1999) describes a similar concept in his three types of coaching conversations that range from building and sharpening a skill to creating a profound and fundamental change. Whitworth writes about the coach attending and listening at three levels: attention on the self, focusing sharply on the other person, and listening to everything that affects the client in her whole environment (Whitworth et al. 1998). My point is that depth coaches need to be comfortable working in all levels and especially, but not exclusively, in the area of transformational change. All levels of coaching and listening are useful *only* if they take the client where he or she wants to go.

For this reason I emphasize the importance that we don't follow a formula, memorize questions, or ask the same questions to each client. Questions must arise from the coach's genuine curiosity and interest in following the client's line of thought and from listening carefully with all five senses to the client's answers (which will in turn lead to further questions). Coaches who follow the hero's journey model will also consider which archetypes a particular client might need to evoke to achieve balance within each stage of the journey and then frame the question accordingly.

Linda's journey. Linda's ostensible difficulty was that she couldn't get started on a marketing plan for her coaching business. After asking several questions (such as, What would it take for you to be ready to market the business?), I noticed that her answers were flat and there was little enthusiasm in her voice. I asked: "How important is the business to you in your life right now? What would it mean to you if you really got this business going? What would that be like?" After several minutes of silence she looked at me and said, "This would mean that I have to grow up and give up my spontaneity and playfulness. I don't want to do that. I don't want to be an adult. Commitment and adulthood feel like shackles and chains." We had reached a deeper level on which to work, where change and transformation needed to take place, where even the goal itself might need to be re-visioned to make room for spontaneity and playfulness to co-exist with commitment and adulthood.

Ingenious assignments. The Magician coach has the task of creating an atmosphere or employing the techniques that make it possible for the client to reach a destination. Even though I emphasize the powerful coaching question, many other avenues to the unconscious and other means to awaken archetypal resources are available. The task of the Magician is to find the appropriate vehicle for each client to carry him to his desired destination. Don't use the same tools and worksheets for every client. Remember that each person has a different path and different talents and responds differently to different modalities. The task of matching each client's learning style and finding special paths to the unconscious is what keeps this job so interesting and exciting.

Use all the ingenious exercises other coaches have devised that plumb the depths and help people change, such as conversations with a future self, and conversations between and among the parts of the self. Use role-play, future searches, dream work, collage making, and rituals that solidify change. For journeys to the Soul, encourage meditation, journaling, prayer, artwork, and any creative endeavor that suits the client. Use the exercises after each chapter. Keep in mind, however, that any of these exercises or any other homework assignments must be tailored specifically to the needs and style of each client. Ask each client to tell you what works and what doesn't.

Ryan's journey. In a workshop Ryan was openly contemptuous of an assignment to create a collage that would represent his desired goals. He thought the exercise was childish and a waste of time. The workshop leader listened carefully and then suggested that Ryan give himself permission to represent his goals in any manner he chose—or give himself permission not to represent them at all. She respected his position and his unwillingness to *do as he was told.* He was acknowledged (found). When that happened he went off by himself and drew a picture of a magical scene that represented his journey and his goals and illustrated the steps he planned to take to reach his destination. He became aware of his power (and his responsibility) to make his own choices and take the actions to get him where he wanted to go. He realized that he didn't have to waste his time being oppositional.

MY MAGICIAN

When I first began coaching I assembled a welcome packet modeled after one I received in my first training program. I also asked each client to email a preparation sheet before each visit that would put the client in charge of the content of the session. I soon found that this worked beautifully for some clients and not at all for others. I have since learned to gather some essential information, suggest some alternatives, and allow clients to take the lead on how they will express themselves.

A big challenge to the therapist who becomes a coach is to learn to ask the powerful questions instead of making statements (which can often be perceived by clients as interpretations and pronouncements). My biggest challenge was learning to change a statement into a question. It is easy to say to a client, "It sounds like you are eager for that to happen," a statement that implies that he or she should be eager for that to happen or that I assume that he is eager. Instead I might ask, If that happens, how will things change for you? or What will that be like?

I must learn to be patient because these questions take time to answer. I have to be aware of my intuition and my hunches but then check them out with clients. If I notice that someone seems angry or sad, I might ask if that is what is going on, if it has anything to do with our session, and if they care to discuss it. Or, I might not mention it at all. I must get clients' permission to enter their kingdoms. I can't assume that I know what clients are feeling or that our relationship gives me the right to invade their territories.

I am also aware of the black-magic danger of predicting how someone will feel. A client reported to me that when she told her psychiatrist about her impending divorce he pronounced, "You will be very sad at some point about this breakup." Instead, a coach might have asked her how she wanted to deal with it or asked, How will you know that you have put this behind you and are ready to take on the new work and change your living arrangements? or What would you need to do to make that happen? Telling her that she would be sad was similar to a post-hypnotic suggestion, a prophesy that would make her feel that something was wrong with her if she didn't feel sad because the expert suggested that she should feel sad. (I fear that I have made many such pronouncements over the years and can only try not to make them in the future.)

I try to lose myself in the session, to focus only on my clients and their needs, to challenge when necessary if something doesn't seem to fit. I must ask for feedback, give feedback, and at all times withhold judgment. At the same time I must not be afraid of holding people accountable to their own goals. That is what they have hired me for.

THE JESTER ARCHETYPE

The ability to experience and enjoy life fully and to tell the truth with impunity.

GIFTS
Joy, freedom, liberation.

ASK YOURSELF . . .
What needs to be enjoyed? Where is the joy and happiness in my work? Where in my life can I *tell it like it is*? Who are the various parts of my personality and how do these parts interact? How can I learn to see my shadow?

THE JESTER: WHAT DO I NEED TO ENJOY AND HOW DO I MAINTAIN BALANCE?

"Fools have a license to say what other people would be hanged for, to puncture the Ruler's ego when the Ruler is in danger of hubris, and to generally provide balance to the kingdom by breaking the rules and thereby allowing an outlet for forbidden insights, behaviors, and feelings."

— CAROL S. PEARSON,
Awakening the Heroes Within

The goal of the Jester is enjoyment and pleasure, yet the Jester is also the part of us who can tell it like it is, the child in the story who was the only one to notice that the emperor was naked. Where is the joy in your life? What do you truly enjoy? How do you play? Are you in touch with your senses? In a slogan attributed to Fritz Perls, "lose your minds and come to your senses," he was invoking the Jester. My favorite image of the Jester is Lily Tomlin in her role as Trudy the Bag Lady in *The Search for Signs of Intelligent Life in the Universe*. Trudy *tells it like it is* and calls reality nothing but a collective hunch and the leading cause of stress among those who are in touch with it (Wagner 1985). The Jester tells us not to take ourselves too seriously. The Jester is Ziggy the cartoon character created by Tom Wilson who tells us, "Never get too personally involved with your own life" (Wilson 1975). The Jester allows us to live in the moment—to celebrate life!

THE JESTER IN OUR PERSONAL LIVES

"The Fool is the aspect of the inner child that knows how to play, to be sensual and in the body. It is at the root of our basic sense of vitality and aliveness, which expresses itself as a primitive, childlike, spontaneous, playful creativity."

— CAROL S. PEARSON,
Awakening the Heroes Within

The Jester opens us up to possibilities, thinking out of the box, and not doing things because they have always been done a certain way. Altering perspectives is a Jester activity. Pearson reminds us that Jung associated the *trickster* with the savior and with inevitable falls from grace (Pearson 1991, 227), leading to the belief that if you always obey the rules you can't begin your own journey. In a previous example, Ryan called on the Jester when he refused to obey the rules and make a collage just because someone told him to.

Although much of coaching has to do with the pull of the future, in contrast to psychotherapy's focus on the past, the Jester archetype is the part that keeps us in the present and enables us to live each day to the fullest. The Jester allows us to play full out, to give it all we've got, right here and right now. "When the Fool is dominant in our lives, we explore the world out of innate curiosity, creating for the simple joy of creation, and living life for its own sake without thought of tomorrow and with little or no concern with convention, traditional morality, or what the neighbors will say" (Pearson 1991, 221–222). The Jester knows how to "be here now." Obviously, the Jester needs the balance of the other Self archetypes, or today will be great but tomorrow will be bleak.

Ask yourself. How is the Jester active in your life? Where do you find joy? How do you play? Think of a time when you were completely present in the moment—right here and now. Are you able to live each day to the fullest (or at least one or two days a week)? We call on the Jester with laughter (not laughter at others but laughter at the absurdity of life) and, at the highest level, with the ability to laugh at ourselves.

We are complex individuals made up of many parts that do not always work together. Have you noticed yourself or others saying things like, Part of me wants to take this job while another part isn't so sure that it is right? Pearson says, "Yet it is part of the human condition that we will experience some radical plurality in our lives: different parts of ourselves, for instance, will want different things. The Fool teaches us to stop denying that this is so and learn to enjoy it" (Pearson 1991, 67).

I think of the Jester as the force or energy that ultimately balances all of the archetypes and helps us achieve inner harmony. Although the Jester is certainly not synonymous with the *shadow*, a most important activation of the Jester is the one that allows us to see our own shadow, or exiled parts, and to integrate previously unknown parts of our personalities. The Jester allows us to express all of the parts of ourselves in the world and achieve yet another form of balance. For that reason I have included the shadow in this section on the Jester.

THE JESTER IN OUR PROFESSIONAL LIVES: THE SHADOW OF THE GUIDE

"If you bring forth what is within you, what you bring forth will save you. If you do not bring forth what is within you, what you do not bring forth will destroy you."

— Jesus,
The Gospel according to Thomas
(from Pagels 1989)

_____

Carl Jung considered the shadow one of the major archetypes in the personal unconscious. We need to be aware of the presence of the shadow sides of both coach and client. The shadow is made up of the parts of ourselves that are unknown to us, unconscious and hidden from the light. When we deny the shadow expression and keep it hidden, it takes on a life of its own and comes to us in dreams, or we project it onto others when we criticize their faults.

While most of the work we do in the Return has to do with more linear, behavioral, and intellectual considerations, some of the deepest work we face is shining light on the shadow. Tendencies to self-sabotage or make negative comments about the self are often evidence of the shadow. The unconscious mind hears what we say and think to ourselves, and negative self-talk becomes the self-fulfilling prophecy we spoke of earlier.

I will leave it to trained Jungian and Freudian analysts to "peer into the dark corners of our mind in which secret shames lie hidden and violent voices are silenced" (Zweig and Abrams 1991, 271). However, each coach or guide, in the course of her own development, must be aware that shadow sides of her own personality may influence her work. In many cases, we may need to help our clients understand how ignorance of their shadows hinders them. And, if it is a legitimate coaching question to ask clients how they contribute to their own dilemmas, then it is a question that we must first have answered for ourselves. If we haven't, we risk sounding like the expert: pontificating, judging, disapproving, or blaming. Even if we are not aware of doing this, it will show up in our voices and manners as we interact with each client. Shadows have a way of doing this.

Frequently we encounter the shadow when we face the fall, when we have been disappointed or betrayed and view dragons as the "other" instead of denied parts of ourselves. We see our shadows projected onto many screens. Hillman says, "Reserves and shadows are not invisible. They show in reticence, in circumlocutions and euphemisms, in shaded averted eyes, in slips, in hesitancies of gestures, second thoughts, avoidances" (Zweig and Abrams 1991, 123). Therefore, we can glimpse the shadows of our clients in their heightened annoyance of the faults of others or lack of awareness of their anger. The job of the coach, however, is not to point out or shine a light on clients' shadows (beware of those who name your shadows for you); the coach can only show clients how to do this for themselves.

Bringing unwelcome thoughts, desires, and negative emotions into our awareness and consciousness doesn't mean we have to act on those thoughts or emotions; nor does it mean that there is something wrong with us for having them. What it does mean is that we can subsequently act intentionally rather than allowing our shadow sides to act through us and subsequently finding ourselves surprised and ashamed at something we have said or done. And remember that the shadow is not all shame and violence. It can contain hidden virtues as well as vices.

Here is one way to think about the shadow. Ken Wilber differentiates between what informs us and what affects us. He says that if something informs us it is not a projection and that which affects us is a projection. He says that we confront the shadow first by taking responsibility for the projection. "The world rejects me" becomes "I reject the world." "Everyone is critical of me" becomes "I am critical of everyone" (Zweig and Abrams, 1991).

What affects you? What do you find objectionable in others? What traits do you dislike? What feedback do you discount or dismiss? Whitworth asks clients to make a mental note of the things they don't want to talk about or think about. She suggests making a simple diagram that illustrates all of the forbidden areas in their minds so clients can see how much time and energy it takes to avoid all of these areas. (Whitworth et al. 1998, 146).

The above is a good example of how a coach can point out what might be a problem and then allow the client to decide what to do (or not to do) about it. A particular client might see that there are areas she avoids and may choose to explore these with a therapist rather than a coach. Others, when made aware of this, will take a stab at looking at these areas on their own. In the process they recognize that they are spending too much valuable time trying to avoid them. What places do you avoid?

The above technique is consistent with depth coaching and similar to the Jungian concept of asking the client to go deeper into the emotion instead of trying to eliminate it, to contemplate a dilemma instead of trying to fix it, to ask what the uncomfortable feeling wants instead of what it means or what caused it. While this work may be uncomfortable, clients are usually willing to do it, for in the end it is productive and liberating and helps them realize more of their potential.

Unlike dragons, who need to be tamed or slain by actions, the shadow simply needs to be bathed in light. I need to be familiar with all of the territory of my journey, and no road must be forbidden to me. If my shadow blots out my righteousness, I won't be aware of it or capable of mediating it with emotional intelligence. If I don't shed light on my sarcastic and thoughtless parts and I pretend I am all sunshine and light, those parts will creep out without my knowledge. Coaches who keep aspects of their personal shadows in the darkness won't be willing to guide clients into those parts of their own personalities that are unknown to them (especially if the clients shadows coincide with the coach's shadows).

The Shadow Ruler

As coaches we catch a glimpse of the shadow Ruler in ourselves when we find ourselves over-critical, attached to success, putting others down, or not keeping our word. The shadow Ruler may show himself in us when we become rigid and regimented in our coaching and coach by the book, or when we strive too hard to control outcomes. In reflection, you might see evidence of the shadow Ruler when you find yourself trying to control the outcome of a session and striving to have the client come away from every session with new heights of awareness and eager to make big changes in the coming days.

Another aspect of the shadow Ruler can be seen in the coach who doesn't take enough power and responsibility in her own professional life but acts like a dictator at home or with friends. Essentially, the shadow Ruler doesn't control those things that are truly hers to control and tries instead to control other people.

The Shadow Sage

The shadow Sage may be so caught up in the world of ideas that she is cut off from her own feelings and disdainful of the feelings of others. Also, in the grip of the negative or shadow Sage, we limit the number of acceptable ways of perceiving reality.

The shadow Sage coach acknowledges only the techniques and methods that correspond with her own learning styles and uses her knowledge as a way to show her superiority to others. She may feel intellectually superior to others and, rather than share her gifts and knowledge, may use her energy to protect her turf. Inside, she may feel cold, empty, and defensive.

We see the shadow Sage in the coach who feels superior to other coaches and is quick to point out other people's deficiencies. Looking back you can see a glimpse of your own shadow Sage when you realize that you have made interpretations and pronouncements instead of asking questions, or when you try to impose the scientific method on a mystical experience, or go to the other extreme and ignore scientific evidence altogether.

The Shadow Magician

The shadow Magician practices black magic by using the knowledge of the human change process to manipulate rather than to guide. When we label, we un-name; when we diagnose we un-name and depersonify through the use of stereotype rather than archetype.

We see the shadow Magician coach in the highly charismatic celebrity coach who dazzles the audience with dramatic and colorful presentations but leaves them feeling inadequate and uncertain about themselves in comparison.

The shadow Magician is responsible for psychological jargon and labeling of clients as narcissistic, or dependent. The shadow Magician is not transparent and keeps her bag of tricks hidden from view. The balanced Magician is open, shares her knowledge with all, and empowers her clients.

The Shadow Jester

The shadow Jester coach is undisciplined and may take advantage of clients sexually or socially. The extreme shadow Jester is a scoundrel who seduces and abuses clients. Other aspects of the shadow Jester appear when coaches don't take clients seriously, when all of life is a joke, and we laugh *at* others instead of *with* them. The shadow Jester is very harmful. Shadow Jester coaches will find themselves entering business arrangements with clients, missing appointments, and not returning phone calls.

My Jester. My Jester is not playful and is not readily evident but shows itself in my sense of humor and ability to enjoy life, find joy in my work, and not take myself too seriously. I enjoy my work and use humor whenever it seems appropriate. I was once very critical of myself because I wasn't playful in the childlike sense (and in turn was critical of those who were—my shadow creeping through). But I know now that just as everyone has a different path, different fingerprints, and different DNA, we each have our own way to actualize the archetypes. I can enjoy the way the Jester comes through wherever I find it. Everyone's Jester is different and each of us plays in our own way.

The Coach and the Jester. Fortunately, I have encountered very few shadow coaches. In general, coaches are outgoing and friendly people who are sincere and open about their work and very willing to share their information, their knowledge, and their techniques with other coaches. Newcomers are welcome in coaching organizations, and I have heard very little judgment and criticism of others. The coaches I have met treat their colleagues in the same respectful way they treat their clients—as peers and equals who have a lot to offer to the world and each other. Professional coaching meetings are a joy to attend and offer an opportunity for personal growth along with an infusion of useful new information—quite a contrast to some other professional meetings I have attended over the years. While it is not all sweetness and light, in general, the Jester archetype is alive and well in the coaching profession.

THE ULTIMATE BALANCING ACT

Shadows are indicative of unbalanced archetypes. To bring the human organism into equilibrium we balance the archetypes. When we operate out of a shadow Ruler, for example, we need to bring other archetypal energies into play to balance his strength. When we find ourselves overbearing and controlling, we need to check out the balance of the Self and see what is missing. We can call on more Caregiver to balance the Warrior with nurturing and self-care and thereby evoke a more benevolent Ruler. When the Caregiver finds herself taking too much care of others, she can call on the Warrior to enforce the rules, strengthen the boundaries, and help provide a more stable kingdom.

The know-it-all Sage can activate the Lover with compassion for himself and others and willingness to commit. The over-dreamy and far-out Sage can call on the Seeker to provide some more practical facts. The manipulative Magician can balance the Destroyer energy with more creativity and imagination. The foolish Jester can ask her Orphan to join with the Innocent and go in search of the Ruler for more order in her life and work.

Balancing the Ego, the Soul, and the Self

The balance of archetypal energies and the dance of Ego, Soul, and Self are examples of a different way to think about a physiology of the human condition. Pearson's archetypes constitute what can be thought of as an anatomy of the psyche. The interaction of the archetypes and the dance of Ego, Soul, and Self are a way to think about the process by which the archetypes interact to achieve psychic homeostasis.

Many of us blindly follow the call of only one archetype or stay stuck in a stage we might have outgrown. Guides and clients alike are often caught in archetypal trances.

A client's journey. I once worked with a woman who was solidly entrenched in her victimhood. She personified the unbalanced Orphan. She had come to me for help in making a decision about her career but had quickly mesmerized me. Granted, her story was a tragic one. Her father abused her when she was a child, and her mother failed to protect her. However, after she left home she accomplished many things and, in addition, spent years in therapy reworking the parental relationship. She was gifted in numerous ways and qualified to work in several interesting professions, yet she remained in a job she hated and in a relationship where she was not valued. As long as I saw her as an Orphan, my Caregiver archetype prevailed, and I treated her as if she were vulnerable. I feared contributing to her problem, and I was concerned that she would not see me as helpful if I held her accountable for her own success. We bumbled along for a while and then one day, as we sat in a gloomy helpless place, I called on my own Self archetypes and asked myself about my responsibilities in this situation. I felt I was slipping into a therapeutic relationship and began to consider referring her to a therapist. I interrupted her monologue and said, "What would it be like if you gave up your victimhood and rewrote the story of your life from the time you left home until now." There was a long silence (which I forced myself to tolerate); then she said, "I wouldn't have an identity. This is the only way I have ever had to define myself. I would have to take responsibility for my own failures, and I am not sure I am willing to do that."

Her words awakened and shocked her. No longer could she say that she had no choice. She had said, "I am not willing. . . ." Like it or not, she had the opportunity to become a hero in her own life and take the journey. I offered to continue the coaching relationship when she became willing to assume her own identity, take responsibility for her personal failures (not the harm that others had done to her), and take credit for her success. Her choice was to return from the journey and take responsibility for her new identity or return to therapy to unhook completely from the past. She chose the journey.

THE DEVELOPMENTAL TASKS OF THE RETURN: INTEGRITY AND GENERATIVITY

"The antidote to exhaustion is wholeness."

— DAVID WHYTE,
Crossing the Unknown Sea

As you can see, the hero's journey never really comes to an end. There are always transitions, new horizons, and new challenges to meet—if we choose to meet them. I have presented a way to think about the completion of essential human developmental tasks by calling on and balancing our inherent inner archetypal resources to accomplish each of these tasks, live a fruitful life, and make a contribution to society. Living from a core of values is living in integrity.

To achieve this balance we must constantly be aware that balance is a conscious act that requires attention and intention; balance and harmony do not happen when we don't play our parts. Think of a juggler balancing many balls in the air at one time. When the juggler is distracted, all the balls come crashing to earth. Each of us is the juggler in our own lives, and we juggle many balls in many systems.

Nonetheless, even though the juggler acts alone, before he got to the place where he now performs, he got help—from parents, teachers, friends, schools, and all of society. None of us do things all by ourselves. We are all a part of larger systems that have produced us and sustained us, and we are components of systems that produce and sustain others. In the Return from the journey we play our individual parts to the best of our ability, always mindful that it is just one part. At the same time we are also mindful that we are

very fortunate to have the opportunity to take the journey. Some in the world must spend so much time in the struggle to survive that the idea of taking the hero's journey is incomprehensible. Others live in such repressive regimes that the very idea of autonomy is considered sacrilege. We, the fortunate ones, have an obligation to be generous with our gifts, to use them and share them with others.

We have been given treasures of enormous value, and most of us meet few obstacles except those we allow to exist within us. I will leave you with this Robert Bly translation of a poem by Antonio Machado:

> The wind, one brilliant day, called
> to my soul with an aroma of jasmine.
> "In return for this jasmine odor,
> I'd like all the odor of your roses."
> "I have no roses; I have no flowers left now
> in my garden. . . . All are dead."
> "Then I'll take the waters of the
> fountains,
> and the yellow leaves and the dried up petals."
> The wind left. . . . I wept. I said to my soul,
> "What have you done with the garden
> entrusted to you?"

At the end of the day, what would your answer be? What have you done with the garden entrusted you? What will you do now that you know it is your responsibility? Where will you start?

Notes

1. Hillman (1996) states that the layers of the state and the strata of the soul are parallel and claims that "what we do in the state we do for the soul."

2. See *Co-Active Coaching*, Whitworth et al., for a comprehensive explanation of the coach-client relationship.

3. The International Coach Federation (ICF) is the largest professional organization worldwide of personal and business coaches. The ethical guidelines of ICF can be found in Whitworth et al., *Co-Active Coaching*, (pp. 170–172) and on the website of the International Coach Federation, www. Coachfederation.com.

4. Schacter-Shalomi explains the Hebrew view of the seven-year cycles of life that relate to the phases of the calendar year. He explains that, in this system, June, July, and August are phases in which mind, body, and heart are unified and says that up to age 49 we

establish responsibility, mastery of institutions, and leadership. Between age 49 and 63, out-growing the need for personal power, we seek to be custodians of the institutions themselves. "Now they can create the magnum opus of their lives. The morning of life is over. . . . This curriculum of life's second half involves more than the completion of our biological imperative. It involves the evocation of soul and spirit." (Schachter-Shalomi and Miller 1995). (23)

5. The basic principles of Appreciative Inquiry are similar to the basic tenets of coaching and are philosophically aligned with the brief therapies and solution-focused therapies that evolved from the family therapy movement.

CHAPTER 3 WORKBOOK

SELF ARCHETYPES

BALANCING THE ARCHETYPES OF THE RETURN

THE RETURN IS WHERE we put it all together. Begin by reviewing your lifeline and filling in or revising any goals that you have for the future. As you work with each of these archetypes, coordinate your action plan with your timeline to help you achieve your goals.

THE RULER ARCHETYPE

In this exercise you will consider your Ruler archetype. Look at your life as if you were the monarch of a small kingdom. As you answer the exercise questions consider your role as the monarch. Are you a benevolent despot or a tyrant? Is your treasury in good shape? Do you need to improve your revenue stream or cut down on expenses? Consider the infrastructure of your kingdom. Is your house in order? Are you doing your part in seeing that the citizens' rights are not violated? Are you taking too much or too little responsibility for the well-being of others in your realm?

Ask yourself:

What is my personal kingdom, and what are my responsibilities to myself?

_____

_____

_____

_____

_____

What is my responsibility to others?

_____

_____

_____

_____

_____

Illustrate or write your role description with respect to your family, primary relationship, work, church, or community group.

_____

_____

_____

_____

Draw a picture of your family as it is now. Who is closest to you? Who is farthest away?

Draw a picture of how you would like it to be. List the steps you have to take to bring the second picture to life.

If you are a coach, answer the following:

In what way are you responsible for the outcome of the coaching process?

_____

_____

_____

_____

_____

What kinds of clients and what kinds of problems are you qualified and prepared to consider?

_____

_____

_____

_____

List three situations you consider to be "uncoachable" and describe what you do when you recognize an "uncoachable" situation or client?

_____

_____

_____

_____

_____

What are you willing to share with the coaching community? What are you going to do about this?

_____

_____

_____

_____

_____

Give examples of situations in which you have found it difficult to maintain your professional boundaries? What are you going to do about this?

_____

_____

_____

_____

In addition to your personal and professional kingdom, what do you owe to your larger community and to society. Are you involved or interested in teaching, professional organizations, volunteer counseling, writing letters to the editor? What are you going to do about this?

_____

_____

_____

_____

_____

The following questions were written with the coach/guide/helper in mind, but they can apply to anyone. There are no right answers, only a hope that each question may lead you to more and more questions and suggest actions you can take to balance your Ego* archetypes.

Think of a way to make a graphic representation of your relationship to your work as if it were the best it could possibly be. What does it look like now? How would you like it to look? What are some of the steps you can take to get from here to there?

_____

_____

_____

_____

_____

How do you set limits and boundaries and make clear contracts with clients about the goals of coaching, the expectations of the client, and the expectations you have for yourself? Give examples.

_____

_____

_____

_____

_____

Ask yourself: How do I set these limits in my personal life? What would my primary relationship look like if I were clear about my expectations and my willingness to participate? What is it that makes it harder for me to set limits in one sphere (home, for example) than another (work)?

_____

_____

_____

_____

THE SAGE ARCHETYPE

In this exercise you will consider your Sage archetype. The Sage asks, What more do I need to learn and how will I learn it? How can I use the wisdom I have accumulated? In the Return we harvest the best of our experiences and find ways to make new mistakes rather than making the same one over and over again.

Answer the following questions taken from the book _LifeLaunch: A Passionate Guide to the Rest of Your Life_ (Hudson and McLean 1996, 110–115).

The adult learning agenda:
What do I need to unlearn?

_____

_____

_____

_____

What new information do I need?

_____

_____

_____

How do I increase my personal competence?

_____
_____
_____
_____

What new technical skills do I need?

_____
_____
_____
_____

How can I stay anchored in my values?

_____
_____
_____
_____

Where are my best learning environments?

_____
_____
_____
_____

Who are my real teachers and mentors?

_____
_____
_____
_____

In addition, answer the following questions.
What areas in your field do you need to or want to learn more about?

_____
_____
_____
_____

If you could study under any teachers (living or dead) or go to any training institute, where and with whom would you study? What are you going to do about this?

_____

_____

_____

_____

_____

_____

_____

Make a list of all of the ways you can keep your Sage alive in your life. What practices do you do to keep your mind and your passions alive? Do you need to learn additional practices such as yoga or meditation to help you keep centered in body and mind? What are you going to do about this?

_____

_____

_____

_____

_____

_____

_____

List your values. Give examples of decisions you have made in line with your values. Looking over your lifeline, what values show up as important time after time?

_____

_____

_____

_____

_____

_____

_____

_____

_____

_____

THE MAGICIAN ARCHETYPE

In these exercises you will consider your Magician archetype. The Magician is an archetype of change. To begin, consider the answers to the following questions. What do you need to change in yourself, your personal life, and your profession? How do you believe change happens? Can people change? How does change come about? What is the coach's role in the change process? What can you change? Now continue with the following exercises.

Make a list of all the things you can change in your life and your environment. List the actions you will take to make those changes.

_____

_____

_____

_____

Make a list of the things you can't change.

_____

_____

_____

_____

Many people are faced with life-threatening illnesses. They are powerless to change the fact of their illness, but they can change their perspective and perhaps even change their lives so that they live each day to the fullest and make the best of what they have. For each situation you can't change, is there any one part of it that is in your power to change?

_____

_____

_____

_____

Years ago I was involved in a research project where we studied the way mothers coped with raising children who had severe physical handicaps. The mothers were faced with children who would never learn to walk and, in some cases, even to speak clearly enough to be understood. A few mothers were defeated by the severity of the problem, but most were astounding. These mothers faced their children's disabilities as challenges and changed everything they could, not the least of which was their perspective and attitude toward the child. They focused on what the child could do, not what she couldn't do, and modified their expectations accordingly.

The serenity prayer that seeks the serenity to accept the things we cannot change, the courage to change the things we can, and the wisdom to know the difference, has been a source of solace for countless people. Accepting the idea that there are things we can't change is important because it frees us to change those things we can. Are you trying to change the unchangeable and neglecting those things in your power?

OBSERVATION EXERCISES

Consider the following questions and suggestions. Set aside some quiet time to review the questions and seriously consider the answers. How do you change your perspective on your desired goals? Do you have a procedure for changing your perspective? Look again at your lifeline. Remember how things looked to you ten years ago? How have you changed perspective since then? Sit on the floor and look at the world from the perspective of a three-year-old. How different is that from the way you see things now? Some people continue to view life from a child's perspective and never take their proper place in the scheme of things. Are there areas in your life where you still see things from a child's perspective? Are there places where this would be a positive thing? Where might it put you at a disadvantage?

For the next few days, give your attention to the following.

Notice how many times in a day you try to change others. What do you want to do about this?

_____

_____

_____

Notice the places in your life where you resist change. Ask yourself, How do I embrace endless change rather than seeing it as something to be resisted?

_____

_____

_____

Ask yourself what you believe about change, the change process, and the role of the coach in helping people to change? What might you have to change about yourself if you take on a different role as a coach and journey guide?

_____

_____

_____

_____

_____

_____

Look at each of your goals for the next phase of your life. List the changes you have to make to attain each goal.

_____

_____

_____

_____

THE JESTER ARCHETYPE

In this exercise you will consider your Jester archetype. Write answers to the following questions. Or if you prefer, set aside some quiet time to review the questions and seriously consider the answers.

What part of your work do you enjoy doing?

_____

_____

_____

_____

How might you bring more joy into your work and your life?

_____

_____

_____

_____

Are there areas in your work where you won't allow the Jester to enter?

_____

_____

_____

_____

Are there areas where you cannot, or should not, "tell it like it is?"

_____

_____

_____

_____

How might you keep your fresh coaching perspective, your ability to see that the emperor isn't wearing any clothes?

_____

_____

_____

How do you keep yourself from taking yourself too seriously?

_____

_____

_____

_____

SHADOW EXERCISE

Although we usually think of the shadow as dark and containing material we regard as undesirable and negative, the shadow can have a positive part as well. That is, you may be keeping some of your positive thoughts, qualities, and attributes out of your awareness. Think back to the section on callings where I spoke of positive projection. Think of the coaches, teachers, therapists, or guides you admire. What is it about them that you would like to emulate? Here is a positive part of the shadow. Often those very qualities you so admire are hidden within you waiting to be awakened.

Then think of people you don't like. Can you find within yourself elements of that shadow as well? All of the characteristics of others are available to you. Bring them into the light. Add them to the mix. You are capable of having bad intentions and good intentions. You are capable of an extremely wide array of behaviors. When you admit this about yourself instead of keeping it a secret from yourself, you can be free to be completely present with others with no fear of their judgment and no need to judge them.

Go back and look at your lifeline. Have you filled in your goals for the time from now to the end of your life? Have you decided how you want to be remembered? Have you harvested the past and learned all the lessons you need? Write a will leaving all of your gifts and treasure to those who will live on after you. Then continue to enjoy these treasures yourself!

_____

_____

_____

_____

_____

_____

EPILOGUE

IN THIS BOOK, I have described a developmental model of the human condition and outlined five steps for a process of coaching that work for me and coincide with my view of the world. I chose the hero's journey and Carol Pearson's elegant archetypal model for its simplicity, its universality, and its emphasis on the need for heroes to return and share their treasures with the community. Because of that emphasis, the model allows us to consider "depth" not only in terms of development from ego to soul to Self, or depth in terms of the unconscious as a source of inner strengths, but also depth (or perhaps breadth) as a description of the way in which we can take into consideration several dimensions of human life—body/mind, soul, and society—in our work with our clients.

As you read the book and completed the exercises, you delved into your unconscious to evoke the archetypal inner resources to face your dragons, to find your treasures, and to discover ways to use your gifts in your work and your life. You also considered the idea of balance in the interrelations of ego, soul, and Self, and the interactions of the archetypes. You learned to consider the importance of using the ego archetypes to do ego tasks and moderate the emotions; the soul archetypes to awaken intention, meaning, and passion; and the Self archetypes to bring forth your essence into your corner of the world.

Now you can apply this to your work with clients. As I continue my work with clients, I find that I must remain mindful of the lessons I've learned and written about here. I have to remember that even though I consciously consider each client as a unique individual, I am capable of having unconscious responses to certain archetypal expressions. Certain unbalanced archetypes, expressed in a client's fears, concerns, or demeanor can elicit my automatic archetypal responses. I've learned that people with unbalanced Innocents can call forth my Caregiver, and unbalanced Orphans evoke my Warrior. When a client seems distressed, therefore, and I am tempted to take care of her or comfort her, I stop and ask myself how I might help her call on her Caregiver for help. When another seems in a downcast Orphan place, incapable of setting limits or standing up for himself, I look for ways to call forth his personal inner Warrior rather than using my Warrior to give him advice or solve his problem.

Thinking of myself as a journey guide and using the five-step process for coaching (outlined in chapter 3) helps me stay clear about my role. Often, when a client begins by asking to work *on purpose* or calling, I'm tempted to set off on the journey without really knowing the starting point. At such times, I remind myself to ensure this client is prepared for the journey ("finding the client") before we go deeper into the soul.

Ultimately, the five-step process reminds me that the journey of the coach is never over—finding myself and clarifying my own point of view is a lifelong adventure that requires lifelong learning. As I write this, the world of coaching is a vibrant and exciting place where people from many fields of study are coming together to share their knowledge to create a useful new discipline. I have tried in this book to present ways to synthesize and organize material from all of these fields in a coherent and complementary way, but there is always more to learn. The journey continues.

GLOSSARY

the hero's journey: A metaphor not only for the chronological and developmental journey through life but also the many forays we take when we leave the familiar behind and venture into a new area or aspect of our lives. The hero's journey is a way to think about the natural history of our species.

the hero: Any woman or man who is free to choose and capable of change.

the call: A yearning or desire for something more in life that *leads* us to leave the familiar behind and begin the journey inward.

the fall: A disappointment, disaster, or other disillusionment that *forces* us to leave the familiar behind and take the inward journey.

dragons: The obstacles (usually internal) that prevent us from setting off on the path to discover who we are.

treasures: The gifts, talents, and special abilities of every individual.

wounds: Injuries to the spirit or psyche inflicted by others.

THE STAGES OF THE JOURNEY

Preparation: Gathering the necessary resources we need to learn to care for, protect, and defend ourselves and function as adults in the world.

Soul Journey: Turning inward to explore, reflect, fight the dragons, claim our gifts, and discover purpose in life.

Return: Taking responsibility for ourselves and others and playing our roles in human society.

References

Adson, P. R. 1999. *Finding your own true north: And helping others find direction in life.* Gladwyne PA: Type & Temperament, Inc. Type and Archetype Press.

Arrien, A. 1993. *The four-fold way.* San Francisco: Harper San Francisco.

Bakal, D. 1999. *Minding the body: Clinical uses of somatic awareness.* New York: The Guilford Press.

Campbell, J. 1968. *The hero with a thousand faces.* Princeton NJ: Bollingen Series.

Campbell, J., and B. Moyers. 1988. *The power of myth.* New York: Doubleday

Carson, R. D. 1990. *Taming your gremlin.* New York: Harper Perennial.

Chinen, A. B. 1989. *In the ever after: Fairy tales and the second half of life.* Wilmette IL: Chiron Publications.

Cole, Thomas R., and Mary G. Winkler (Eds.). 1994. *Oxford book of aging: Reflections on the journey of life.* New York: Oxford University Press.

Cooperrider, D. L., and P. F. Sorenson, et al. (Eds.). 2000. *Appreciative inquiry: Rethinking human organization toward a positive theory of change.* Champaign IL: Stipes Publishing.

Cooperrider, D. L., and S. Srivastva. 2000. Appreciative inquiry in organizational life. In *Appreciate inquiry: Rethinking human organization toward a positive theory of change.* D. L. Cooperrider, P. F. Sorenson, D. Whitney and T. F. Yaeger. Champaign IL: Stipes Publishing.

De Shazer, S. 1990. What is it about brief therapy that works? In *Brief therapy: Myths, metaphors and methods.* J. K. Zeig and S. G. Gilligan. New York: Brunner/Mazel.

Egan, G. 1998. *The skilled helper: A problem-management approach to helping.* Pacific Grove CA: Brooks/Cole Publishing Company.

Ellis, D. B. 1998. *Creating your future.* New York: Houghton Mifflin Company.

Erikson, Erik H. 1963. *Childhood and society.* New York: W. W. Norton and Company, Inc.

Flaherty, J. 1999. *Coaching: Evoking excellence in others.* Boston: Butterworth Heinemann.

Freidan, Betty. 1993. *The fountain of age.* New York: Simon and Schuster.

Fritz, Robert. 1989. *The path of least resistance.* New York: Fawcett Books.

Goldenson, Robert M. (Ed.). 1984. *Longman dictionary of psychology and psychiatry.* New York: Longman.

Goleman, D. 1995. *Emotional intelligence.* New York: Bantam Books.

Hampden-Turner, C. 1982. *Maps of the Mind.* New York: Macmillan.

Hargrove, R. 1995. *Masterful coaching: Extraordinary results by transforming people and the way they think and work together.* San Francisco: Jossey-Bass.

Havens, L. 1988. *Making contact: Uses of language in psychotherapy.* Cambridge MA: Harvard University Press.

Hillman, J. 1992. *Re-visioning psychology.* New York: Harper Collins.

———.1996. The soul's code: In search of character and calling. New York: Random House.

Hudson, F. M. 1999. *The Handbook of Coaching: A comprehensive resource guide for managers, executives, consultants, and human resource professionals.* San Francisco: Jossey-Bass.

Hudson, F. M., and P. D. McLean 1996. *LifeLaunch: A passionate guide to the rest of your life.* Santa Barbara CA: The Hudson Institute Press.

Johnson, R. A. 1986. *Inner work: Using dreams and active imagination for personal growth.* San Francisco: Harper & Row.

——.1991. *Femininity lost and regained.* New York: HarperPerennial.

Jung, C. G. 1960. *The stages of life.* In *The collected works of C. G. Jung.* Vol. 8. Princeton NJ: Princeton University Press.

Kopp. S. 1972. *If you meet the Buddha on the road, kill him! The pilgrimage of psychotherapy patients.* Palo Alto CA: Science and Behavior Books.

——. 1988. *Raise your right hand against fear: Extend the other in compassion.* Minneapolis MN: CompCare Publishers.

Leider, R. J. 1997. *The power of purpose: Creating meaning in your life and work.* San Francisco: Berrett-Koehler.

Leider, R. J., and D. A. Shapiro. 1995. *Repacking your bags: How to live a life with a new sense of purpose.* New York: MJF Books.

——. 2001. *Whistle while you work: Heeding your life's calling.* San Francisco: Berrett-Koehler Publishers, Inc.

Lesser, E. 1999. *The new American spirituality: A seeker's guide.* New York: Random House.

Levine, S. 1997. *A year to live.* New York: Bell Tower.

Levoy, G. 1997. *Callings: Finding and following an authentic life.* New York: Three Rivers Press.

Milne, A. A. 1926. *Winnie the Pooh.* New York: E. P. Dutton & Co., Inc.

Moore, T. 1994. *Soul mates: Honoring the mysteries of love and relationship.* New York: Harper Collins.

O'Hanlon, B. 1996. *The handout book.* Omaha: Possibility Press.

O'Hanlon, B., and S. Beadle. 1999. *A guide to possibility land.* New York: Norton.

Pagels, E. 1989. *The gnostic gospels.* New York, Vintage Books.

Pearson, C. S. 1986. *The hero within: Six archetypes we live by.* San Francisco: Harper & Row.

——. 1991. *Awakening the heroes within: Twelve archetypes to help us find ourselves and transform our world.* San Francisco: Harper Collins.

Richardson, C. 1998. *Take time for your life.* New York: Broadway Books.

Rico, G. L. 1991. *Pain and possibility: Writing your way through personal crisis.* Los Angeles: Jeremy Tarcher, Inc.

Robertson, R. 1992. *Beginners guide to Jungian psychology.* York Beach ME: Nicolas-Hays, Inc.

Rogers, C. R. 1961. *On becoming a person.* Boston: Houghton Mifflin Company.

Roszak, T. 1998. *America the wise: The longevity revolution and the true wealth of nations.* New York: Houghton Mifflin Company.

Schachter-Shalomi, Z., and R. S. Miller. 1995. *From age-ing to sage-ing.* New York: Warner Books, Inc.

Sher, B., with A. Gottlieb. 1979. *Wishcraft: How to get what you really want.* New York: Ballentine Books.

Stevens, A. 1982. *Archetypes: A natural history of the self.* New York: William Morrow and Company, Inc.

———. 1995. *Private myths: Dreams and dreaming.* Cambridge MA: Harvard University Press.

Stone, H., and S. Stone. 1993. *Embracing your inner critic.* San Francisco: Harper San Francisco.

Storr, A. 1988. *Solitude: A return to the self.* New York: The Free Press.

Vaill, P. B. 1996. *Learning as a way of being.* San Francisco: Jossey-Bass Inc.

Wagner, J. 1985. *The search for signs of intelligent life in the universe.* New York: Harper & Row.

Weisbord, M., and S. Janoff. 2000. *Future search.* San Francisco: Berrett-Koehler Publishers.

White, M., and D. Epston. 1990. *Narrative means to therapeutic ends.* New York: W. W. Norton & Company, Inc.

White, T. H. 1987. *The once and future king.* New York: The Berkley Publishing Group.

Whitmore, J. 1996. *Coaching for performance.* London: Nicolas Breadly Publishers.

Whitworth, L., H. Kimsey-House, and P. Sandahl. 1998. *Coactive coaching: New skills for coaching people toward success in life and work.* Palo Alto: Davies-Black.

Whyte, D. 1992. *Fire in the earth.* Langley WA: Many Rivers Press.

———. 1994. National Public Radio: Fresh air with Terry Gross. Princeton, NJ: Spencer Entertainment Enterprise.

———. 2001. *Crossing the unknown sea: Work as a pilgrimage of identity.* New York: Riverhead Books.

Wilson, R. 1975. *Never get too personally involved with your own life.* New York: Sheed and Ward, Inc.

Zweig, C., and J. Abrams (Eds.). 1991. *Meeting the shadow: The hidden power of the dark side of human nature.* Los Angeles: Jeremy Tarcher, Inc.

index

A

adult development x, 1

appreciative inquiry 79

archetype
     definition 3–5

Arrien, Angeles 78

B

balance 4, 7, 11, 16–17, **30**, 45, 51, 69, 71, 72, 74,
     95–96

Barken, Barry 82

boulders 41–42

C

call 2, 37–41

Campbell, Joseph vii, ix, 2, 37, 41, 43, 45, 51

Caregiver 4, 5, 6, 10–12, 15, 17, **25–26**, 28, 32, 72, 74,
     95

Chinen 81

Creator 4, 5, 6, 35, 48–**51**, **67–68**, 84, 88

D

dependence 2, 3, 5

Destroyer 4, 5, 6, 35, 40–46, 48, 51, **61–64**, **69**, 95

Dragon 41–43, 44, 62

E

Ego 2–5, 6–8, 16, 17, 21–22, **28–31**, 36, 45, 46, 51, **69**,
     71, 72, 78, 95, **104**

Erikson, Erik 1, 2, 3, 5, 8, 72, 81

F

fall 2, 9, 21, 37–38, 93

Flaherty, J. 89

Fool 4, 91, 92

Freud, Sigmund 2–3

Fritz, Robert 49, 91

G

gifts 2, 6, 42, 50, **58**, **67–69**, 81, 96, 111, 113, 115

gremlins 41

H

Hargrove, R. 76, 84, 89

Havens, L. 87

Hillman, James 37, 52, 71, 93, 96

Hoffer, Eric 82

Hudson, Frederic x, 36, 75, 79, 82, 83, 89

Hudson Institute of Santa Barbara x, 75, 83

I

independence 2, 3, 5, 7, 8, 16, 72

Innocent 3, 4, 5, 6, 7–9, 10, 15, **22**, **23**, 95

inner child 14–15

inner parent 15–16

Institute for Life Coaching, The x

interdependence 2, 3, 5, 9, 72

International Coach Federation 77, 96

J

Jester 4, 5, 6, 91, 92, 94, 95, **110**

Jester/Fool 4